AMBERSHORE
By Rhoda Gurevich

Synopsis.

The heavy Russian boot tramples the dreams of the youngsters of Riga, Latvia.

The Nazi locust eats its way through Europe. When the war reaches Latvia in 1941, the innocents of the country ask which is worse the Russians or the Germans?

A Riga teenager jumps onto the last train out of the city to an unknown destination. Raised with love, nurtured by the sun of a Latvian resort called Ambershore, she will confront a world of hunger, lies, pain and death. She is the amber of the Baltic, as fluid as a resin-drop from a rooted pine tree becoming hard and strong and golden.

For nearly four decades waves toss our heroine closer to a shore. It is not Ambershore of her youth that she approaches, but the shores of freedom, the American shores.

The life of Rhoda Gurevich, is filled with family, friends and enemies, each of whom provide her with life experience and give her the courage she needs to endure a thirty-six year life of Russian hardship.

The book is laced with extravagant smells of home made bread, smoked fish from the European open-market, twisted with the human smells of close contact in cattle cars and escape. Our appetites are whetted with a boiled potato and little salt.

This is yet another story of roots, representing all of our ancestors who strove for a better life for their unborn children. It is another story of escape to freedom and the individual odyssey that it took to get there. But as we are all alike, our individual struggle is unique.

The heroes in Gurevich's book are women: her mother who gave her grace and courage; the grandmother who taught her wisdom; the teenage girl who forced her family to flee the Germans; her Aunt Eva who fed her in the hungry years; her daughters who made her realize the need to escape. And finally, Rhoda herself, whose passion and perseverance saved her life and the life of her family. Rhoda who had the courage to take the risk when she approached a KGB colonel for the help she needed to become liberated from Russian oppression.

Acknowledgment:

My thanks to Andrea Tobias and to Sandra Hersh, my teachers whose English training and editing assisted me in making this book. To my children and my grandchildren, who are my strength, my love, the meaning of my life. Above all to the most important person in my life, my greatest friend, my husband Pinkhus.

Dedication:

To my mother and my father.

PROLOGUE

Riga, Latvia: June 17, 1940

Goodbye my beloved Hamora school, adieu childhood... What is ahead for me? In these thoughts I hear a key rotate in the door. I run to the entrance, my father's hazel eyes glow with joy, he hugs me and plants a kiss on my forehead.

"Rodinkah, you are accepted to the "Ivrit Gymnasium," you are a big girl now, you became a gymnasium student."

"Here's mamochka coming!" I cry out in excitement.

"Anna, the competition was enormous, but our daughter received all fives at the entrance exams. I committed to pay three hundred lat tuition per year."

My arms wrap around my mother's neck, scattering kisses on both of her cheeks.

"Mamochka, I am a gymnasium girl already, will you buy for me black patent-leather pumps on a three centimeter heel?"

"My dear child, congratulations," she kisses me back, "this kind of shoes you will get when you turn sixteen."

"Mamochka, I'll have to wait for two more years, gymnasium girls are wearing shoes on a heel when they are fifteen. By winter I will be fourteen and a half, this is close to fifteen."

I paint my future in the new school: new teachers, new students, some of my old friends.

I am inpatient to wear my new uniform and then the gymnasium beret made of blue velvet with a golden stripe instead of the black one with silver. The Ivrit Gymnasium! How proud I am. There is nothing that could shatter my blessedness.

"Tomorrow is Mina Tzimerman's birthday party. Could I stay late?"

"Who will take you home?" Both my parents ask in one voice.

"Ilja Avin and Vulya Sternin will bring Adya Vinnik and me."

"It is all right if you go all together, you are a big girl now," my mother says jokingly.

Next evening we are returning from the party giggling and cheering.

What is going on there? Why are the streets crowded with people?

Vulya, as usually, comes up with a joke, "They are all accepted to the Ivrit Gymnasium as we are, so they celebrate."

"Vulya, what happened to your voice, it sounded normal in school, are you hoarse?" Adya laughs.

"His voice is changing," Ilja smiles. "Vulya, you are going to have a bass."

As we approach the railroad square, the masses are growing. Our curious boys run into the crowd to find out what is going on there. They return swiftly like different people; all their childish comfort is gone.

"Adya, Roda, listen: "Soviet tanks crossed the Latvian borders, they will be in Riga by tomorrow."

"What is going to happen?"

"Who knows?"

Our dreams are shattered, intuitively we pick up our pace and before I know it, I am running. My thoughts frighten me; only at the end of last summer, on September the first, 1939, when we remained for Rosh-Hashana at Ambershore, the Germans invaded Poland. Now, nine months later, the Russians invade Latvia.

"Goodnight guys. Adya, I'll see you in the morning." I run quickly upstairs and ring the bell. My father opens the door.

"Thank God, you're home." He pulls me close to him. My mother is distressed, the socialist in my father thinks it is all right, Uncle Marcus, my mother's brother who lives with us, predicts trouble.

"Go to bed, my child, it is late," my mother brushes through my hair. I cannot fall asleep, I feel restless. In the morning, I want to go to Adya's, but my mother would not let me out of the house by myself.

"Anna, I will take the child to the railroad station," Marcus says.

"Yes, Uncle Marcus, let's go."

It is hard to pass through the dense forest of people. We finally approach the station and watch tank after tank pulling into the ample square.

"Yes... These are the Red Army tanks," Marcus says with a heavy sigh.

Within the crowd there are groups of excited well wishers so impatiently waiting to receive the Red Army with bright-red roses.

"Zdravstvuyte, Tovarishchi: Welcome, Comrades," they shout as they throw the roses at the soldiers.

Other supporters reach out with their placards for the Red Army liberators.

"Why are these people so happy?" I ask Uncle Marcus.

"Those are the members of the underground Communist party, they have opened the political jail to liberate their comrades, look how proudly they are carrying them in their arms right to the tanks. Remember my words: there will come a time when they will become disappointed."

There is no resistance. The tankists are brave to jump out of their tanks and fling themselves into a Russian dance "Kalinka" accompanied by the music of a harmonica.

"It's time for us to go home, the air is heavy, the situation is dangerous." Marcus whispers into my ear.

We return home to the bad news: after we left, Latvian nationalists along with the police got into fighting with Soviet soldiers who had pushed a few of the police officers into the canal near the railroad station.

Next day, Latvia has acquiesced: she is a small country with only six tanks; no match for the Soviet monster. Shortly after, a new government, headed by August Kirchenshtein, has been established. It takes hardly one month when on July 21, 1940, the Latvians ask Moscow for acceptance into the Union, as do Estonia and Lithuania. I witness history as the Soviet Union gains three more Republics bringing the number to fifteen.

****

The Soviet Latvia closes down our Hebrew schools, only Yiddish schools stay open. My beloved teacher, Mrs. Vinnik, tells my mother that it is no point to send us to the Ivrit Gymnasium, they would teach in Yiddish anyway. We will send our children to the "First Yiddish Gymnasium" where our Hamora teachers are hired.

September the first: I am dressed in my new navy blue uniform, with a white silk collar and cuffs edged with laces, a white pleated apron above my dress. I carry an autumn bouquet of fresh cut flowers in one hand, a new brown leather brief-case in the other hand. The city bus, number thirty-four, takes me to school.

My first day in the gymnasium! Right away, I sense a different atmosphere: the Zionist spirit is gone, replaced by Communist ideals. My Hamora teachers speak Yiddish instead of Hebrew, they look dreary and tense. The new teachers are more relaxed. Still, the level of education is very high. I spend the long winter nights studying, there are two new subjects added to our gymnasium curriculum: the Russian language and the History of the Communist Party. Slowly, I become accustomed to my new life, so do my old friends.

Spring is around the corner with its long awaited excitements of our exams (I love mathematics taught by Mr. Zvi Gram), our outing and our graduation.

Finally, the happy day arrives, our class is going to the picturesque Sigulda called the Latvian Switzerland. We dress casually, rucksacks on our backs, and we are ready for the big adventure with the awesome head-teacher, Israel Brown.

****

We return home tired but happy in the anticipation of our graduation party. I can hardly sleep that night. In the morning, I exchange telephone calls with my friends. At last, it is time to go to the party. I enter the hall with my mother by my side. Everyone looks festive, so do I in my new navy blue pleated silk dress; the orchestra is playing and our girls are dancing with the shy boys. Vulya invites me for the "Blue Donau" waltz, we swing, we dance the Lambeth Walk, we dance and dance … My mother is in deep conversation with other parents, everyone is wondering:

"Where is Mrs. Vinnik?"

"I do not see Adya either."

"Why is the ceremony delayed?"

A rumor snakes its way through the crowd: Israel Brown has been arrested (he is a socialist), more rumors … Mrs. Vinnik along with her husband and Adya are also arrested (they are Zionists). All of them are confined to trains which will exile them to Siberia.

"Why?" We ask in shock. The hall becomes petrified with fear. We are too afraid to stay, too afraid to go home.

These are no rumors, this is the truth. The following days we learn of more families that begin to disappear; the Soviets accuse them of being political and economic threats to the Communist Society.

Riga starts to whisper, everyone is scared, the people begin hoarding food, but the KGB sets strict reprisals on hoarding: immediate arrest and confiscation of property. More news; the stores empty of food, of clothing, of footwear, of everything…

My mother sends me to buy soap: I stand in a long line for two hours from where neither the start nor the end could be seen.

"They are out of soap," I hear a voice, I return home empty handed.

Next day, my mother rushes to buy shoes for me. There are no patent-leather shoes of my dream anymore. We go from store to store until we find a pair of soft maroon leather sport shoes, my mother is in disbelief when the store manager asks for her passport to mark our purchase.

Little did I know then that these would be the only pair of shoes I would wear for the next four years in the muddy falls and the bitter cold winters.

****

Thunder! Thunder! Thunder!!!

A compressed human voice, the voice of the Moscow News Broadcasting anchor, Levitan.

"At dawn, on June 22, 1941, without warning, the German Air-Force treacherously assaulted the peaceful Soviet skies by way of the Baltic Republics."

CHAPTER I

THE TRAIN TO SOMEWHERE

Riga, Latvia: July 27, 1941

Everyone from our five-story building runs to Kaplan's flat on the first floor. We sit troubled, not knowing what is going on; parents keep asking each other: "why is it so quiet, after five days of intense bombardments?" Unexpectedly, Grieze's eighteen-year old daughter, Lyolya rushes in and cries out in a hysteria:

"We have to go to the train immediately. The Germans are close."

She continuous yelling instinctively: "we have to leave, we have to go…"

We trust her insight and without lingering my mother, Uncle Marcus and I run upstairs to our apartment; we throw some clothes into a suitcase, lock the door and leave our past behind us. There is no time to alert our relatives; the telephone communication is cut off and it is dangerous to go to their homes. (It would not be until four years later that we would learn about their fate.) Along with the Griezes, the Shperlings, the Baranovs, the Kramers and the Kaplan's son we leave the house. We hardly turn onto Gogol Street, when from a roof-top heavy shooting begins. The Latvian fascists seize two loaded trucks of

Russian guns which the Red Army supplies the Guard to defend the city; these guns had been constructed and manufactured in 1891 by Mosin: the only guns the Soviet Union possesses at the beginning of the war.

The fascists go to various neighborhoods and from the roofs shoot at Jews who try to escape. We are forced to return home, but this energetic eighteen-year old Lyolya would not let us remain in Riga; she convinces us to try again. The second time we get through, and finally reach the terminal. From far away we still hear shooting, now it becomes stronger and more frequent. The Latvian fascists are shelling us from across the street, from the roof of the Belevue Hotel. Everyone lies down on the floor of the terminal when suddenly a voice cries out:

"Run ... run to the trains, forget about tickets!"

When we reach the railroad tracks, there are two trains on different platforms. One is empty; the other is already overcrowded. There are hundreds more passengers pushing to get on, trying to jam into the full train. We do the same, but the people at the door are pushing us back. I see a Russian soldier near an open window inside the car.

"Please, I beg him, pull me through the window."

He drags me into the car. I am a beautiful teenager—perhaps this gives me clout. Once inside I force myself to the door and drag in my mother and Uncle Marcus from the platform. My father is not with us: he has been called into the Red Guard to defend the city.

We are on a train to an unknown destination, so squeezed in that we can barely remain standing. We have neither food nor water, it is impossible to get to a toilet. When the train stops, a crowd bursts out and runs into the woods for relief. No one knows when the train will leave. When it does start again, the passengers run to catch it; some of them are not lucky to make it back. The ones who are left behind are fated with six million of their brothers and sisters.

Ivanovo

Still in Latvia, local people bring pails of milk for us. "Don't touch it," we are warned by an unknown voice, "it is poisoned by the fascists." The train moves slowly, and with all the stops and starts, we loose count of the days. When finally we reach a safe place where bombardments can no longer be heard, we begin to settle into actual moments of relief which allow us to think about the sweet life we left behind.

Our train pulls off to a railroad junction; it is an ancient Russian city established in the twelfth century, and named after the Wise of Kievan Russia, Yaroslav, now an industrial and commercial center. Here we are finally given food after four days of hunger. The next stop is Ivanovo, a city of four hundred thousand, a center of the Russian cotton-milling industry. We get off the train and are taken to a collective farm, a place where we weed fields ten hours a day and collect nothing for our work. However, we are given food to eat and real beds to sleep in. The fresh air and the meal of potatoes with bread and milk tastes to us like a royal feast.

The first summer of the war, the summer of 1941, is very successful for Hitler's army. The Germans open several fronts in the Soviet territory and advance rapidly in all directions until they are soon near Moscow. The Russians continuously dismantle the heavy machinery factories in the prefrontal zones, they ship them hurriedly to the Urals and Siberia to expedite the production of armaments: tanks, planes and later the famous Katyushas. A massive evacuation of the population is going on at the same time.

We also are ordered to evacuate by Ivanovo officials. Back we crawl, this time into closed cattle cars that would take us deeper into Russia. Once again we are traveling as far as we could to Who-Knows-Where.

Laughter and Waves: The Music of Ambershore

Our train is pulled off many times at either railroad junctions, or branch lines in order to let the ever-moving transport of the Red Army soldiers and ammunition proceed to the front. The guns have priority over the evacuees. The journey that would usually take no more than five days in peacetime takes us a month in wartime.

At major railroad stations we are given food. Otherwise the trip is uneventful. Day after day I lay in the dark slow moving slatted train. As the wheels turn monotonously, my mind wanders into the comfort of my past.

I remembered another steam locomotive, which pulled railway cars filled with happy passengers going to the shore. Husbands rushed to spend Saturday nights and Sundays with their families in rented cottages; those who could not afford the rentals pressed to the beach early Sunday morning for the day, returning home tanned and relaxed late at night. It took an hour to reach the most populated resort: Ambershore. We, children, vied for the window seats. Shortly after the train left the station with its shrill whistle, I watched the expanse of the succulent green forests. Within a half hour we would arrive in Priedaine, the Latvian name for pine. These pine trees with their shallow roots exuded through their green needles a specific scent of resin, so pleasant...so pleasant to remember. I knew from my natural history lessons that even a minute injury to a pine tree, a small wound made by a wood-pecker, or a broken branch on a windy day would bring about resin to ooze. We were told that too much pressure inside the trees' resin passages forced droplets to the surface of branches and of the trunk itself causing these little droplets of refracted sunlight to break into rainbows of colors, and give off the clean fragrance of pine. Certainly, a big contrast with the putrid smell of our now unwashed bodies in the cattle car. The piney environment was thought to have curative powers for the lungs, so much so that on the advice of their doctors many people spent summers in Priedaine, the last stop before the stretch of beaches started.

As the train breezed along the track, I anticipated the bridge over the Lielupe River. From then on, the passengers could count on getting a seat. I craned my neck to look at each terminal as the train stopped, trying to catch glances of what other girls were wearing. I liked their shorts and bare shouldered tanks. Their mothers usually wore white or navy jersey slacks with striped tops. The cast bronze tans on their skin indicated the good times they were having. Three more stops and we would reach Ambershore.

Soon I too could change into my beach clothes. The train emptied even though there were at least eight more towns to go through. Ambershore, however, was the most popular resort of them all with a shore line extending to over thirty kilometers of beach with pine-lined dunes, sand so soft, so fine that each tiny grain tickled your feet as you treaded upon it. The water in the bay was shallow. We walked and walked and thought if we walked far enough we would reach Sweden, the water was as cold as on the coast of Maine. However, in the evening the bay warmed up a little by the sun of the day. It did not matter what time it was. From early morning until late night, the beach was alive with lovers, with husbands and wives, with children, their arms linked together in friendship. We played volleyball, we jogged, we bicycled. Laughter and waves: the music of Ambershore.

Here different groups of Jewish teenagers met, bound by the languages they spoke, by the schools they attended. They were all snobs: the German-speaking thought they were the elite, the Russian-speaking thought they were the ones, the Yiddish-speaking thought they were the ones, and the Hebrew-speaking knew they were the ones.

****

It was here that I met my friend Tanya. When I first saw her, she was riding a bicycle. Her long blond hair fell down onto her shoulders, and looked even lighter against her cast bronze tan. Her hazel eyes, broad cheekbones, and slight turned-up nose could have caused traffic accidents when the boys would spin around to look at her. But there was no traffic. Tanya was always laughing, a habit that made her even more beautiful. She had a strong body and was always dressed in the style as defined by the fashion magazines of the mid-thirties: a short pleated skirt showed off her tanned legs when she ran. She wore "Beck shoes" which were lightweight sneakers made from white kid, edged in blue.

It was 1937. Shirley Temple dictated our styles; Hitler dictated other styles. Both styles crossed different oceans. In Paris, Picasso had just painted Guernica, another manifestation of Hitler's style. However, at that time we children were occupied only with Shirley Temple.

In appearance and demeanor, I was the antithesis of Tanya. I had long black hair and was tall. Tanya was lighthearted, while I took things more seriously. We both were the only children. We were the "Rigans." We were the elite. Riga was known as the little Paris of the Baltics and was thought to be the center of culture, intellect and style. The spirit of Riga was expressed through its rigorous education system in school and its strict upbringing at home.

Tanya and I spent entire days together. I liked to listen to her play the piano songs we knew, singing together in all the languages we spoke. We tangoed; we waltzed; we loved swing, and we danced the new hit the Lambeth Walk. This was our rock and roll. We worshipped the pastries in the cafes. Needless to say that our love for "creamschnidts" did not keep us slim. But then, slim was not the style: zaftig was.

Like all best friends, we exchanged clothes for the day; we ate in each other's homes, and we laughed at the silliness of the boys. We knew each other's parents and were close to them. My mother kept a strict eye on who my friends were, so I was grateful that she allowed our friendship to blossom.

Our fathers' professional lives were intertwined as well for they were both in the lumber business. However, in the early thirties, during the Depression, the over-industrialized Latvia experienced decay. The bankruptcy of Germany's Donatbank led to the closure of all German banks. Shipments of Latvian lumber to Germany were halted; consequently our fathers lost their jobs. Germany looked to its economic solution in the Nazi party which was heavily financed by German millionaires Hugenberg, Kirdoff and Schroder. At the time that Hitler seized dictatorial power, Karlis Ulmanis became president of Latvia. The credit crisis in Germany resulted in a withdrawal of credit reserves from Latvian banks. Only a banking moratorium saved the country's financial position from downfall. Being Minister of the Farmers' Union before, Ulmanis directed his full attention to the rise of agrarian interests in Latvia; the land with its energetic farmers continued to increase its efficiency; the agraricultural output found greater demand from export markets, and along with lumber and its by-products revived the Latvian economy. Ulmanis changed the political structure of the country: the Latvian Saeim, represented by delegates of more than twenty parties was dissolved. The concentration of power in the hands of the new President, enhanced Latvia's economy, but at the same time gave rise to Latvian nationalism. The lumber business improved in Riga, and my father started to earn a good living again. My mother was relieved and could once again direct her full attention to my upbringing.

****

The train to Who-Knows-Where chugs on. In my innocence, I want the bad to be over. I want to go home. In 1995, I still hear my mother's voice asking: "Ven vet kumen an end tzu dem"? The voice of everyone. "When will this ever be over?"

Still August 1941

As the train bumped the Volpyansky's into an unknown future, on the other side of the globe, in Washington DC, The National Gallery of Art opened. Who was to know that fifty years later, another museum would open several blocks away memorializing the Holocaust that I was going through.

****

I listened to the voices in my head of happy Augusts past; the times when I visited my father's cousins Eva and Jacob, and their three children: Chona, Rachel and Ben in the small town of Varaklyani. I could not know then that my life with them would become braided like a challah, sweet and tight.

On Fridays in Varaklyani, farmers were bringing their produce to the market. Later in the day, you could see them in their heavy boots walking on Riga Street where one shop lined up next to the other. Somewhere in the middle was Uncle Jacob's fabric store. Since Jacob knew that I was a responsible child, he relied on me to handle the cashier's desk on that busiest day of the week. Later he permitted me to cut the cotton scarves from the bolt, a luxury in great demand by the farmers' wives. I hugged and kissed him for his trust and remembered his strong arms responding to my gratefulness. I remembered also his smell of perspiration and muslin. In the afternoon, when business slowed down, Uncle Jacob would give me one lat, a lot of money for a young child in the late nineteen thirties. I ran to the candy store with Rachel, this coin clasped covetously in my hand.

Every male Jew was a king in his home on the Shabbat, his wife--an exhausted queen. The men would slowly walk to the synagogue for services and return home to their festive dinner tables. At that time the streets became empty until one-by-one old and young would gather for a walk to the only park in Varaklyani, "Der Deutsche Veg." On Sunday we went bicycling and stopped at the river to swim with Rachel's and Ben's friends. But the great fun was still ahead when in the evening we so proudly went to the big dance party on the green, at the Latvian gymnasium. The Latvian youngsters were tall with blue eyes and blond hair. I loved watching them dance to the music of the town's firefighters' brass band: Latvians and Jews together. Even though I was younger than they, I too was invited to dance. I could not then imagine that these Latvian youngsters could murder their Jewish friends ever ... ever.

****

It had already been two months since we fled from home. I was grateful that I was not alone and that my Mamochka was next to me. The cattle car came to an abrupt halt bumping me back into the present. The dust and dirt that the train raised, the unwashed bodies made me feel even worse for my mother than for myself.

By nature my mother, Anna Volpyansky, was an immaculate person, both about herself and about our home. Her measure of success was that you could see your face reflected in the dust-free highly polished furniture. Our home was not only impeccably clean, but it was stunningly done in the new style called "Art Deco," all custom made furniture. The design in the walnut wood itself stood out from the brown lacquer; the chairs were upholstered in royal blue grosgrain; a large crystal basket edged in silver, and Rosenthal china gave our room a look of elegance. I also remembered the soft gray shade of wood in my parents' bedroom and the salmon-colored satin, lined in silk, bedspread. I felt at peace when I entered this room.

I thought there could be no nicer furniture than in my parents' home. (After the war, at Riga's huge flee market one could find beautiful household goods from china to furniture. Sadly, for the most part these were items stolen from the Jews who were forced out of their homes to the ghetto.)

The Farmers' Market

My mother was an excellent cook. At that time, there were no refrigerators in the homes, we had to shop at the Central Farmers' Market for fresh food every day. The market was recognized as one of the best in all of Europe. It was a place, which captured melting smells, colors, textures and sounds. For one thing each pavilion was contained under a giant glass roof. Not only Latvian but also Lithuanian farmers came to sell their fresh produce here.

There was a fish pavilion equipped with huge fifty gallon glass tanks filled with silver carp, white fish, pike, bream and trench. I liked to watch my mother choose a fish from the fishmongers who pulled them out of the tanks with a net bucket. Many times, to my delight, the fish were so vigorous that they jumped back into the tanks, splashing water onto the floor and putting a show on for me. I would turn my head away from the small Latvian crayfish that moved slowly on the tank's bottom. I could not look at them: was it because they were so ugly, or because they were "treif?" Neither did we buy the smoked slender eel, or marinated lamprey which was kept in small wooden barrels. They too were treif. We proceeded further. Each time we approached the next section, my appetite was whetted by the fresh smoked smelts with their golden skins, the delicious smoked baby flounders, the lox, then a great delicacy, with its thick pink meat under spotless curved glass covers apart from all other displays.

Whole carcasses, and fresh cuts of beef, veal and lamb hung on large hooks in the meat pavilion. We knew that the meat was fresh because the animals were slaughtered the night before. The butchers looked like surgeons in their snow-white overalls; the meat cutters were in the background in their blood spotted rubber aprons. The Latvian reader may be aware that I have omitted pork in this description. Of course, there was pork and bacon. It was a staple in all Latvian Christian kitchens, but I feared the page would burn beneath my fingers because of our dietary beliefs.

My mother did not buy any meat at this open market. On our way home, we would stop at Dumeshe's kosher butchery, on Gogol Street, where my mother selected veal or beef briskets, cutlets, tongues or calves liver. She did buy live poultry at the market to bring to the slaughter house right there, where the birds were slaughtered and de-feathered on the spot in the kosher way.

In the summer, the Baltics enjoyed the harvest of various berries: strawberries, blackberries, raspberries, red and black currants, gooseberries and red bilberries used in large quantities to make preserves. My mother cooked the bilberries with sour apples and small pears, and stored it in large glazed clay pots for the winter. Apples and pears of many varieties; yellow and blue plums from the new harvest, appeared in August.

There was another pavilion where dairy was sold: the home-made farmers' cheese and yellow cheeses with caraway seeds were displayed on trays; sour cream and sweet cream, stored in white enameled pails; bricks of home-made butter with a slight aroma of almond, were in great demand by the Rigan consumers. Here you could buy large loaves of country-style rye bread and sourdough bread baked from the rich grains grown in Latvian fields.

The farmers would also bring white and yellow eggs just laid by the chickens, so beautiful were the eggs that the yolks stood up. We liked to make a hole in the shell and drink from the thick golden liquid.

Golden was the honey of various flavors and shades, and the honeycombs that resembled our amber; appropriately called by the people—Latvian gold.

****

Family

Again, I fell asleep into my memories. When I awoke my empty stomach screamed and gurgled from hunger. I craved for something of my mother's cooking. In my mind I saw her as she was then, two long months ago - another lifetime ago. In the evening, when my father arrived home, she dressed as an Empress for her presentation of the dinner. In the winter, my father would bring home exotic fruit from Richter's specialized store: oranges, grapefruit and bananas in neat paper bags tied with a thin strong braided string, dates and figs in long narrow boxes.

At dinner my mother would tell him about her day and my scholastic successes. He glowed with pride, and nodded for me to come over. I sat down on his lap in anticipation of the kiss he would plant on my forehead. There were many kisses, and I know now that it was their great love for me and for each other that gave me the strength to go through the trials I was to experience later.

Both my mother and father were tall, handsome looking people: she with hair of chestnut brown, swimming in highlights of cooper; black alert eyes filled with intelligence that held the secrets of the universe. My father was a gentleman, energetic, all business, serious and very responsible. He was a socialist, she a strong opponent to leftists' streams. I cannot remember political discussions, (they were few); I do know that what came out of these two strongly oppositional parents was a daughter, their only child, who became a fiery Zionist in her beliefs and actions.

My parents were outgoing people. You could see them in the theater, in the opera-house and in a restaurant, dining with friends. When they were out for the evening, I was taken care of by my Uncle Marcus, who came to live with us after his wife had died. He was in his sixties, with a trimmed beard, short in stature, with a small body muscular from miles of walking, When I think of Uncle Marcus, I see him rush to the synagogue twice a day; I hear his voice singing the blessings over the wine and the challah at our Shabbat table. I also remember his hands like two birds, fluttering and flying with imagery and metaphor, hands that made stories come alive. As he tucked me in at night he would say:

"Machucha e Babulya, good night."

"What does that mean?" I always laughed.

"It means what it means," he said, "now go to sleep."

But I wheedled out of him more time to stay up.

"Sit next to me, and tell me another story." I pleaded.

He could never say "No" to me. He fed me stories as a mother-bird feeds her young. I swallowed them hungrily, a taste here, a bite there. He told me all about family history and about people I had never met. But he did it with so much humor and passion that I couldn't get my fill of them.

****

Originally, the Raikin family came to Riga from the town of Polotsk in Belo-Russia. Later on, part of the family moved to Petrograg. When in 1918, Latvia gained independence from Russia, the strict rules under the Bolshevik regime did not allow any connections with a foreign country. This way the Raikin family lost contact. Thanks to Marcus' stories I was later able to trace my relatives, most importantly my first cousins: Raya, Lily and Semyon, the children of my mother's brother, Uncle Max. I never saw him, for when I arrived in 1957 in Leningrad to finally meet my family, he was already dead.

With all the stories Marcus told me about relatives, a cousin, Arkady Raikin, a young comedian, sprung out as the most colorful and later, nationally famous when more than two hundred million people would smile and nod in acknowledgment at the mention of his name.

Uncle Marcus told me that my grandmother, Nechama Raikin, came from a Rabbinical family by the name of Rabinovich. My grandparent's wedding was a "shidach." Then parents would arrange a match between two families to assure that the "iches" of both was right. Nechama met Solomon under the wedding canopy for the first time and for the rest of their lives.

It was right.

My grandmother lived to be eighty: at that time considered a long life. I did not remember my grandfather because he died much earlier than my grandmother. Like her son Marcus, Nechama was also short, but her wise eyes made her look tall. People used to come and ask her opinion on various matters because they knew she had an innate sense of wisdom. For instance, when cousin Olya asked her.

"Nechama, should I inquire of my sister Genya to send me a shifscartte ?"

My grandmother would nod her head. This body motion was her answer. It took Olya a few years, and she was on a boat to America. Friends and family came to my grandmother with real and profound situations: marital problems, emotional problems, financial problems. Zhenya, Uncle David's daughter, asked her:

"Why does Simka, my father's wife, control the money that my brother Littman sends from South Africa?" My grandmother answered arms raised in supplication, "There should be peace in the house."

My grandmother protected my childhood secrets. At times when my mother did not permit me to wear my new shoes to school, I went to her. I would ask my grandmother to let me go to a friend after school, she answered with a wink. Later she convinced my mother in her own way that it was all right. Nechama was always meticulously dressed in silk or fine wool with a jabot to cover her bodice. To me she was a queen.

****

One cold winter night as I lie next to her on her goose feather bed covered up to our noses with a down comforter, she says to my mother: "Bring an orange for the child." Then she says: "Look how the skin of your hands is cracked from the cold, put on glycerin."

My grandmother steps out of her bed to use the night potty. My mother follows her with her eyes. My Babushka collapses before her.

My mother screams. Then she realizes that I am watching. "Take the child to Mrs. Brown," she has the presence to command. The next thing I remember, I am lying in our neighbor's white and starched bed that smells of fresh air. My father comes to see me next morning. He does not take me home until the funeral is over. When I return, I rush to open the dresser. I look at my grandmother's dresses and smell her sweet powdery scent. Now when I remember my little Babushka, I remember her beautiful black eyes that held the knowledge of the world: eyes that made her look so tall and me feel so loved.

****

As the train chugged along, my thoughts kept rhythm with the rolling wheels. Faster and faster came the fluid beat. Uncle David danced before me with his tall lithe body. He was really my grandfather Solomon's cousin, but my mother called him uncle. He lived near us, on the corner of Kurmanova and Dzirnavu Streets. Often on my way home from school, I would run in just to say hello and get a candy. David's first wife died but he remarried a woman called Simka the iron fist-in-a-velvet glove. I can still see the long gray braid that hung down her back, in contrast to old David's gray beard that hung down in front of him like a mop-head. Except for Zhenya, none of his three other children was around. David was a lonely man.

Eingemachts:

[A JEWISH DESSERT FOR HOLIDAYS]

Peel the skin of two pounds black radishes.

Grind radishes with tin grater.

Soak grated radishes in cold water for twelve hours,

Change water three times.

Dry radish in paper towels.

Boil a pound of honey with one and a half glasses of water

In a stainless steel pot stir constantly with a wooden spoon.

Add grated radish and simmer until golden brown.

Throw two handfuls of almonds in a separate pot of boiling water for five minutes.

Rinse with cold water and remove skins.

Add peeled almonds and a dash of ground ginger,

Cook for ten more minutes.

Serve cold in a footed crystal vase.

Eat in small dessert plates with forks and loved ones.

The holiday of "Simchat Torah" was celebrated with great delight in our home. The table was richly laid with a variety of Jewish-style foods, wines and desserts: "Eingemachts, Tayglach and Ingberlach, " all Jewish traditional sweets. We could not celebrate a "Simcha" without Eingemachts or Uncle David, the joy bringer. After a good drink, humor poured out of him. Once, I remembered when he climbed onto the table and danced: a cherished image that warmed me to this day. It seemed that Arkady, inherited his grandfather's artistic skills.

My mother shook me from my daydreams. Uncle David and Arkady danced away from me in a haze of sharp awareness.

"Get up, my child," she said, "we are approaching Kuybishev." I sat down swiftly on a wooden bench next to my mother and Uncle Marcus, who either napped or sat silently most of the trip. There were rumors that we would be getting off at Kuybishev, a city of over a million people on the Volga River. But when we approached the terminal no one ordered us to leave the train. The echelon manager announced that we will stay here for a few hours. We could, however, step out and take a short walk. My mother permitted me to go with our neighbors, she gave me a three ruble bill to buy ice-cream. Holding the money tightly in my fist, I ran non-stop until I found an ice-cream stand, but so did everyone else. A long line of people was moving vigorously; soon I was close enough to get my ice-cream. The moment I opened my fist that was holding the money, someone snatched my three ruble bill. Tears began to run down my cheeks; my steps became faster and faster as I rushed back to the train. Shall I tell the truth to my mother? I had never lied to her before. When my mother saw the expression on my face, she asked me of what happened. She was upset and lectured me about being more careful next time. Uncle Marcus came to my defense.

"Things like that happen when there are so many hungry people."

The lost ice-cream was not the only disappointment I suffered that day. Since they were already overburdened with evacuees, Kuybishev did not accept us. Our train would have to move deeper into Russia. My mother saved the poor meal of watery soup and bread that we were given. I became already used to the tasteless food; it still filled up my belly. For the rest of our trip, I kept hearing "Tashkent, Tashkent," but I did not recognize the word. Finally, it was told to be our next home.

Within six months "Tashkent" and sorrow were one word.

As the train moved again, I lowered myself onto the floor, curled up into a frightened bundle, and started floating in my dreams. My sleep must have been deep and long, for when I woke up, we were close to the Steppes of Kazachstan, in the Asian part of the Soviet Union. Each time we stopped, I saw strange looking people who spoke an unknown language. We were still far away from Tashkent having enough time to think about how we would adjust here in Asia. I saw my mother become more exhausted and sad. I had to take responsibility and made a promise that I would apply all the knowledge from my excellent education to support us.

My strength was always in mathematics. I was a mathematical genius, and liked to solve problems. Little did I know then, that my education was more valuable than gold, especially here where my life would become a complicated series of problem solving.

****

Education in Latvia

For it was a port of entry from the Baltic Sea, Riga always attracted its powerful neighbors. At various times in the Latvian history beginning from 1201, Latvia was ruled by Poles, Swedes, Germans and Russians. These countries fought many battles for having control over the possession of Latvia. As one country of conquerors was replaced by another, it left its people behind. Thus Riga collected many nationalities along with many languages and diverse cultures. The radical change from the Bolshevik Revolution in 1917, along with the confusion in World War I in 1914-1918, resulted in the withdrawal of the aggressors from the Baltic countries. Latvia, Estonia and Lithuania found themselves finally free from German and Russian occupation.

After seven centuries of foreign domination, Latvia was eager to become independent and take its place in the European community.

In their homes, people chose to use a language according to their background and their philosophical convictions. It was not uncommon to speak more than one language. Traditionally, Latvian Christians sent their children to Latvian-speaking schools. Russian, Polish and German parents sent their children either to schools of their native language or to Latvian schools. However, the Jews, being concerned with their past in Latvia, made radical decisions in choosing education for their children.

Up until the 1840's, Jews were not permitted to live in Riga. They had been ostracized to the near-by town called Sloka. When finally Jews settled in Riga, they were allowed to build synagogues, own real estate and engage in trade.

Riga became the economic, political, cultural and social center for Latvian Jewry. Through the democratic regime of the country from 1920-1934, they represented various fractions in the Saeim: like the Ultra-Religious, the Zionist and the Bund. The latter was a Jewish Social-Democratic union all through Europe which represented the minority position in the Bolshevik Revolution. The Bund demanded to be recognized as the only representative of the Jewish proletariat. When the Saeim was dissolved in Latvia, the Ultra- Religious and Zionist organizations were legally allowed to stay active. The Bund movement, however, being a threat to the country's political system, was forbidden. Nevertheless, its philosophy remained alive which has been conducted from the underground.

There were parents who sent their children to Yiddish schools where liberal ideas such as equality and economic concern for the poor had been espoused. Yiddish, also the original language of the wonderful literature by Sholom Aleichem, Sholom Ash, Itzhak Peretz, Mendele-mocheir-sforim; the language of the colorful drama, comedy and melodrama became the most popular tool for educating the young. Other parents preferred Jewish schools where the instructional language was Russian, German or Latvian. There were ultra-religious Hebrew schools; like "Torah Vederech Eretz" and "Tushia." And two other excellent Hebrew schools; "Ivrit" which Tanya attended and "Hamora,—my beloved school. All of them provided high quality education. Together with the parents, the schools shaped a Jewish intellectual society.

Malka and Leib

Today my memories were making me as sad as they used to when Passover was gone.

I remembered the anticipation of spring, the anticipation of Passover when my paternal grandparents, Malka and Leib would come to Riga from the province to celebrate the holidays with us and with their other children and grandchildren. Fifteen people would gather around the table for the celebration of the Exodus from Egypt: the first night at Aunt Yacha's comfortable home, the second night in our lovely home.

My father's mother Malka, was tall and regal, which was what the name "Malka" meant. She was sixty-four. While she sat in a chair, I would stand behind and with her comb arrange her long gray hair; she must have loved our times together since she always gave me permission to go on by nodding and smiling. Then, there was my grandfather Leib, an energetic person who had his own small business manufacturing turpentine. He was quick-witted and intelligent, eyes alert to the landscapes around him. Not only did he like to test my scholastic abilities, but he always wanted to know how my mind worked on other matters.

"Kum aher tsu mir," he would motion with his hand for me to come over. He hugged me telling that I was a "lichtike kop." I wanted Passover to continue forever. I wanted Malka and Leib to live forever.

After Pesach was over, I lay in my bed thinking about how quickly good times come to an end. I remembered wondering of what would come after the pleasant moments in life; thoughts which filled me with fear. Finally, I fell asleep, and of course, as the night melted into day, so did my childhood worries.

****

But where could I escape now? It was most difficult to wake-up in the morning here on the train, and realize that this uncertainty had become our reality.

CHAPTER II

TASHKENT

Six Months In Hell

If the reader remembers, Kuybishev did not accept us. Tashkent, the capital of the Soviet Uzbek Republic, could not accommodate us either. As all cities, Tashkent was already overflowing with evacuees, therefore special committees were organized to deal with the resettlement of the huge number of the homeless. While waiting for further orders, our train remained at the Tashkent terminal. I noticed three young men at the railroad platform whose names I found out later to be Misha Halsband, and two brothers, Mulya and Natan Gordon. They looked familiar to me: Misha was wearing a pajama top, instead of a shirt, because he did not have one. That strange outfit made me remember seeing him at the Ivanovo terminal. These three men joined our group as they too were from Latvia. The committee sent our little crowd of Rigans to an Uzbek village called Rishtan, in the Fergana Valley.

Although the origin of the Uzbek nation has not been clearly established, it was thought that they were of Mongol-Turkish ancestry. Their facial configuration, high cheekbones, light brown skin color were unfamiliar to us. They spoke Russian with a stilted accent, their own Uzbek language sounded totally foreign to us. It was August 1941, an unusually hot August, the temperature read above a hundred degrees, but the Uzbek men wore heavily quilted cotton robes, their heads were covered with small pentagonal-shaped embroidered caps. These men spent most of the day in tea rooms sitting on clay floors which were covered with richly designed Oriental rugs, sipping green tea, cup after cup, a way they found relief from the heat. We saw the Uzbek women only in the market place; we could not see their faces which were covered from head down to the waist with heavy black "Paranja." These women did not speak Russian at all. In spite of the way we felt about the strange Uzbek language, the way the people dressed, their looks, we were pleased with the warm welcome we received there.

They settled our group in a cozy tea room where we were to sleep on the floor. The next day we all went out to seek employment; we needed to buy food. But the drastic change in the climate made many of us ill with malaria and dysentery - customary diseases in that area. Of course, we were trouble to the local people; but the war was a common disaster for the entire Soviet population. Needless to say, we looked as strange to them as they did to us and they would come to the tea room to observe us. Among the Uzbek men

there was a woman who spoke Russian. She was a Bucharian Jew. Within one week, I came down with dysentery, and had been admitted into a fifteen-bed hospital. My mother and Uncle Marcus remained in the tea room.

One day, my mother came to visit me in the hospital with news about the Bucharian woman who showed up in the tea room again asking for me. She wished to help us; she was the chief accountant in the only tractor-machinery station in Rishtan. They had apartments available for their employees, and if I was good with numbers she could hire me as a bookkeeper-trainee, she said. How was I to know then that she also had other plans for me? I was thrilled with the good news. Becoming so eager to take on this job, I recovered in two days. My mother picked me up from the hospital and took me directly to our new apartment. What a surprise, it had hardwood floors! We knew from our Riga friends that not everyone was so lucky. Most of the evacuees were living on damp, cold clay floors without rugs. Our simple clean studio with a kitchen seemed a gift from heaven.

Comrade Rubinova, as she was called, hired me to do the bookkeeping. Thanks to my mathematical skills, I could handle my duties easily without much training. One night, she invited me to her apartment for dinner. I hadn't had a good meal since we left Riga. Anticipating the visit as if I were a starving kitten, I still was disappointed that my mother and uncle could not share my good fortune.

A steaming hot lamb pilaf with snow white rice was served on beautiful china; the Rubinovs ate this kingly repast with their fingers. Since childhood, my mother taught me to eat holding the fork in my left hand and the knife in my right hand, so I could not even imagine to eat their way until Yefim Rubinov insisted to feed me with his fingers. He was a teacher, the brother-in-law of comrade Rubinova. They were trying to make a match. I was fifteen; he was twenty-six. I felt awkward and shy and knew with every bite that my family was hungry.

Bucharian Jews were similar in tradition to Sephardic Jews. They did not speak Yiddish but they knew how to pray in Hebrew and even though they looked like Uzbeks, they were still Jews. However, nothing was more important to me at the time than the meal.

Two hours later, I returned from that rich home overcrowded with opulence and Oriental rugs, to our empty and hungry home, filled only with worry and love.

One day, the young teacher invited me to the movies. I felt uncomfortable to go, I felt guilt to refuse. Some fear entered my mind for I had heard that young women in Asia matured faster than in Europe. What did he expect of me? I was suspicious of comrade Rubinova's motives. Then there was Misha Halsband who felt affection for me. He wrote poems with messages saying, "Wu bistu, libste, fun my blick farshvunden?" [Where did you disappear from my glance, my darling?] He was three years older than I. I felt flattered that he cared for me, however, not always without disappointment: he sometimes missed our Rigans group gatherings. On these occasions, Misha would tell me that he had to see "someone," but said that I was too young to ask questions. He was right; did I need, in my innocence, to know that it was a woman with whom he could pleasure himself?

Misha Halsband was soon called into the army, and, as so many others, killed.

More and more evacuees started arriving in this Uzbek village of less than ten thousand people. They were from various regions of the Soviet Union: Moscow, Leningrad, Kiev and other cities where they were lucky to escape Hitler's attrocities. We noticed them to be already familiar in the ways Soviet system worked. It might have been to their credit that these people could deal with the formidable reality more easily than we did. Their harsh Soviet experience equipped them with talents far beyond ours, which enabled them to survive in any possible way. We were innocent and had to learn to develop survival skills. We did not know about the black market; we did not know how to network, neither did we ask for help. We were reticent about complaining, we suffered in silence.

29

One day, after two months of living in the luxury apartment, Yefim yelled under our window for me to come outside. He had to talk to me, he said. I walked out.

"What did you say about me?" He demanded.

.   "What are you taking about?"

"You know very well what I'm talking about," he shouted as I shrugged my shoulders.

Then he asked again.

"Did you meet a woman with two daughters who evacuated from Kiev?"

"No," I said.

"You must have noticed them. The village is small and one of the daughters has been an eye-full. She was eighteen and gorgeous."

Ah! I finally caught on. Someone had created a story about me.

"I never had a conversation about you with anyone." I defended myself.

Either he didn't believe me or he didn't want to believe me but I responded to his accusations by bursting out into tears and ran away home. When my mother and Uncle Marcus asked me what happened, I could hardly explain for the tears. I finally collected myself and told them the story; my dear mother figured it out immediately.

"Don't cry, my child. You did nothing wrong. You have been framed. "Der lebn is nisht farflantst mit rosen," she continued, "this story was made up by people who want to harm us. The woman from Kiev with her daughters want this apartment. My dear child, you have to become strong and learn to overcome injustice."

A week later we were asked to leave, and the mother with the daughters from Kiev moved in on top of us, even before we could find another place to go. I never talked to the teacher again. I heard that he was soon called into the army. He did not survive the war.

****

A couple from Lithuania, also evacuees, agreed to share their one room cabin with us. As fall approached, our dwelling became bitter cold. There were no rugs to cover the clay floor; no wood to heat the room. If we were warmly clothed; if we had a cozy hearth; if we had enough to eat; the deep cold fall would not have been a burden. But we were poor, cold and hungry without hope. All we had was the love and empathy we felt toward one other. We had nothing to furnish the half room with. Our first apartment had beds in it, but we were not permitted to take them with us—we had only old blankets, given by the Uzbek people, to cover the floor for the night to sleep.

More and more evacuees started arriving, the cost of food began to increase daily. Prices rose ten-fold within four months. Because fruit was cheap, that was all we ate with freshly baked pita-bread. Before the convergence of the evacuees, we could buy grapes, apricots, cantaloupes, watermelons. We would cook a soup using dried fruit instead of meat. Now we could only afford white radishes with onions for a salad and our ration of bread that came undercooked. We were not able to figure out how to make a living with the little money we made. We saw that some evacuees were selling bread on the black market. We did not know where to get the bread or how to start profiteering. Besides, if you were caught, you were arrested. We remained in our cold cabin, there was no place for us to go to warm ourselves. Cold and hunger became our constant companions.

****

On January 10, 1942, Uncle Marcus did not wake up. I pushed and pushed him, but he did not respond. My mother rushed over to touch him.

"Motl, Marcus, wake up! My dear brother is dead!" she cried out hysterically.

It was impossible to bear the sadness I felt to lose this beloved person who threaded my entire childhood with love and humor. Now, we had to make arrangements for his funeral, but we did not know where to start. The simple Uzbeks came to our aid; I understood then that all people carry goodness within themselves, especially at hard times like we had experienced.

CHAPTER III
CHEBOKSARY: 1942
My Mother

The sisters, Sonia Bushkin and Gitta Russ, also evacuees from Riga, tried to persuade my mother to leave Uzbekistan and go back to the Russian Republic. They learned that a Latvian Division within the Red Army had been formed and stationed in a village called Gorochovetz, near the city of Gorky . Both women were looking for their husbands as we were—for my father. They kept insisting that we would all find our loved ones there.

My mother became depressed from everything that was happening to us since the beginning of the war, so she finally gave into these women's hypothesis. The women each with their two little sons, my mother and I were ready for this journey. We were given permission only to travel as far as Cheboksary, about six hundred kilometers away from Gorky: Gorky was off-limit for its close position to the front line.

The winter of 1942 was the coldest people could remember. Thanks to this unusual 1941-1942 bitter-cold Russian winter the Red Army stopped Hitler from approaching Moscow. The Nazis planned a "Blitz Krieg." Instead they had to confront the Russian severe frost for which they were unprepared physically or mentally. We too did not anticipate the consequences of our senseless adventure. We sold some of our clothing which we dragged along in our only suitcase, and bought rail-tickets. We were going back the same way as we came: through the Kazachstan Steppes and the Ural Mountains. We were already in the bitter cold Urals, when suddenly, our train-car stopped and remained standing on the tracks. The rest of our train proceeded long ago. The passengers were not informed what was happening until we were ordered to leave the car. They disconnected us because the car and all its passengers had to be disinfected. As we learned, a man who had been taken to a hospital from our car had contracted typhus. We all had lice as a result of the anti-sanitary conditions and from exhaustion.

We were next to the station of Chkalov. The bath was at the terminal where we washed ourselves thoroughly, so was our clothing decontaminated. We had no towels to dry ourselves; we put on the warm clothes on our wet bodies. In the bitter cold we ran back to our train car, but the sanitation team would not let us enter for they had not finished cleaning yet, so we rushed back to the terminal. It was closed too; it was like a curse to us that it was being sanitized at that very time. Everything turned against us. Where were we to go? We had no other place besides the outside bitter cold. I remember my mother shivering as she tried to shrink into herself as a protection from the cold. I remember wanting to help her warm—wanting to protect her. I remember my own cold.

When we were finally called to the train, my mother was burning with a high fever; as the night approached, I watched her condition worsen, unfortunately I was helpless to ease her suffering. It must have taken a long time before we arrived in Chebokasary. My dear mother was taken to a hospital right from the train where they diagnosed her with pneumonia. They sent me to a shelter for evacuees. Still cold and shivering I did not know how to warm myself. I moved closer to a little stove in the middle of the room. The heat comforted me until I smelled something burning. The people next to me began yelling:

"Your coat is burning!"

This was my only coat, now with a burned-out hole. I could hardly wait next morning to run to the hospital to see my mother. Her condition did not improve; they did not have effective medicine to take care of her; penicillin was not then available yet.

They warned me in the shelter to find a place to move to. I ran back and forth in the strange city in the bitter cold without warm clothing; visiting my mother in the hospital, and looking for a place to live. A week later, I became ill with typhus. My high fever made me unconscious and could hardly remember how I got to the hospital. When I did regain conscious awareness, I saw that everyone in my hospital room was with shaved heads, I looked around at a room full of bald heads. My hand shot to my beautiful thick black hair. "Oh, God," I screamed out. I too was bald. For a moment I forgot my mother, and felt the vanity of a teenager. When I came to my senses and asked a nurse about my mother, she never answered my question. I asked my doctor, but she too would not talk about my mother. So, I decided to write a letter to my dear mother in hope that someone will deliver it to her. Luckily, I noticed a nurse whom I recognized to be from my mother's ward. She agreed to take the letter. I waited for an answer. There was none. My condition improved and I would soon be out of there. Next morning I tried to get up from bed, but my feet would not move. My legs were covered with big red spots. The doctor came into my room, she looked at my legs and ordered a consultation for me. I was diagnosed with a post-typhus heart complication and was transferred to my mother's ward. First, the nurses gave me a bath. When I asked them about my mother, they ignored my question and went on speaking in the Chuvash language which I did not understand. As they brought me to the hospital room, I recognized a patient, an evacuee from Moscow, who spoke Russian. At my request about where my mother was, this woman did not give me any information. I had a premonition of bad news already and now her silence made it even worse. The days came and went but I could find out nothing.

One night in May, a week before my sixteenth birthday, a nurse entered my hospital room. I did not know her.

"You might remember a woman by the name of Anna Volpyansky here."

The nurse responded immediately:

"She died upstairs in surgery when they tried to remove fluid from her lungs," she continued, "this poor woman had a daughter who suddenly disappeared; she asked everyone in the hospital to help find her child."

"I was the daughter," I burst out in tears. "I was sick with typhus here in this same hospital."

That spring night, confined to a hospital bed far away from home, having just lost my uncle, having no knowledge of whether my father was alive, I lost my only hope, my dear mother. Each footstep behind the door reminded me of my mother's steps. I felt that she would enter my room any minute. I pictured her being happy, back in Riga, then again sadly carrying the burden of the war. I knew that I had lost her forever, but I just could not accept it. However, my young and strong body helped me to conquer my illness. My doctor permitted me to get out of bed where I was cofined for a whole month after another month before that in the infection ward. In the long narrow hospital corridor I saw new faces. I started to feel hungry again, but there was no place to get food. The patients around me were all suffering from hunger the same as did I; these were the people whom

I shared with the first burning pain of my loss.

The hospital was ready to discharge me. I feared this moment for I had no place to go. I became used to the hospital. I could not figure out how to start life without my mother. When the day came to leave, I got dressed into my clothes. With a broken heart and weak legs I took step after step up to the next floor to the surgery. I asked a nurse to tell me about my mother, but she was unfriendly, she did not tell me anything, even the date of her death. Instead she sent me to the morgue. There, besides my fear, I could not find anything or anyone else. I returned back to surgery. But they again just sent me to the morgue. So I left the hospital not having any knowledge of the date my mother died and of the place she was buried. I keep her memorial in my heart. I observe it in accordance with Jewish law on the day when I learned of her death.

My mother was a source of power and inspiration to me, the closest person in my life. Her philosophy of love and the importance of family was strong and is carried on through generations.

Life, I thought then, must go on and hope should not be lost.

Now my immediate goal was to find my father.

Destiny

Since childhood, I have believed that a person's life is predestined by a higher power; the important thing was how I would interpret its voice.

Four months after I left the hospital, I received a letter from my Aunt Eva. They were lucky to escape from the Nazis in Varaklyani and find a safe haven in a small forested town north of Gorky. Were it not for that letter, who knows what would have happened to me. I did not have enough food to eat to gain strength after my illness. The loss of my mother and uncle and the uncertainty of whether or not my father was alive, were thoughts that I always carried with me. I was just sixteen and already tired and worn down, not only from grief and illness, but from loneliness. Still I knew that I had to pull myself together.

.   *********

Here in Cheboksary, I found Mrs. Kahn, another evacuee from Riga who worked for an organization that supplied the army with food and clothing. She was an earnest woman in her late thirties who listened with great concern to my story. She said that she knew who I was since she and my parents had had common friends. Within three days she had arranged for me to work as a trainee in the sewing shop. She could do no better because she was only a cashier. However, the organization offered great benefits: they had a cafeteria to feed dinners to their employees. Of course, I accepted this job immediately. The people in the sewing shop, most of them evacuees, were amicable and taught me how to sew. As a group we would go to the cafeteria and joke at the dinner table pretending that we were at a banquet even though we were still hungry. Occasionally we could afford to go to a commercial cafeteria for lentil soup sold without ration coupons. Still it was guaranteed that your stomach will remain empty.

Recipe

Lentil Soup:

Buy three portions of watery soup.

Pour out the water of two soups,

Combine the lentils with the third soup.

My mother always said that everything was "bashert." So, on a spiritual level, it was no accident that when I opened the door to this cafeteria, there before me were several other evacuees from Riga, Kraslava and Rezekne. Two sisters Sonia and Rosa Schtamler looked at me with curiosity. Not because they recognized me; not only because I was a new face, albeit a hungry wan looking face, but this little face beneath a shaven head looked as if she had just come out of a concentration camp. They did, however, recognize the people I was with since they had met previously. I was the new girl in town. Naturally, they asked me questions and I answered. We were bound together in our plight for I was Latvian as were they. The good-hearted sisters immediately offered their support; first I was invited to a "potato party."

Recipe

Boiled Potatoes:

Take a broken pot,

A wooden spoon,

Boil two quarts water

Throw a few wrinkled potatoes,

Eat with a sprinkling of salt.

At their home I met Sarah, a young woman, who had recently moved to Cheboksary from a near-by collective farm. I found out from her conversation that more evacuees from Latvian towns still remained on that farm.

"Are there people from Varaklyani?" I asked her.

"Yes, Leib and Eda Yoffe," she said

"Leib Yoffe!" I exclaimed, "he was the principal of the Yiddish school which Rachel and Ben attended."

"Yes," she nodded. A nod that made a great difference in my life.

Sarah gave me the Yoffes' address, and it was not long after that I received a letter back, that my relatives had escaped from the Nazis. He closed his letter with my aunt's address.

My Aunt Eva's letter filled me with excitement and warmed my lonely soul. She wrote:

"My dear Rodinkah,

It was hard for me to recognize the

teenage girl whom I knew so well and saw just a year ago.

Stones could break from the pain you went through in
this long year.

Don't worry anymore, you will come and live with us.

There will be enough bread and potatoes for you.

You won't be alone anymore.

I love you, Eva. [S lyubovyu, Eva]

All my sadness melted into endless tears of happiness. Along with the letter my aunt sent me money and a travel permit.

The days became damp and cold. Cheboksary, a city on the Volga River was drenched with rain. Autumn had begun; the rain poured continuously. My first impulse was to run to share this news with the Schtamler sisters. In order to get there I had to cross a clay hill; as I walked, my feet sunk heavily into the wet slippery clay, and the only pair of shoes I had stuck in the soil each time I took a step. I cherished the worn out shoes as if they were made of gold, the shoes my mother had to sign into her passport. I finally made it over the red mud. The sisters received my good news as if it were theirs and immediately started to help me plan the trip to my relatives.

The terminals were packed with hungry civilians; soldiers were relocating from one front to another. We were cautioned about theft and rape in the terminals and on the trains. The journey promised to be long and dangerous for a young girl. So, the sisters suggested that I take a boat to Gorky in order to avoid all the train connections and from there proceed by train to my destination. That very night my grandmother Nechama came to me in my dreams and warned me not to go by boat. I followed my grandmother's guidance. After two weeks of preparations and another three days of traveling, I finally arrived in a tiny place called Obchod.

CHAPTER IV
OBCHOD
Eva and Jacob

I could smell fall in the air. In contrast to Cheboksary, close to Siberia, autumn was clean and crisp; the smell of leaves in the breath of the cool wind was filled with wood and pine.

It was well past midnight when I stepped into a dimly lit terminal. A cashier sat behind a small window. Since the train from the opposite direction had not yet arrived, she let me in, otherwise the terminal would have been locked. There was no possible way of communicating my arrival to my relatives, so I followed the instructions in my aunt's letter and waited until morning. I felt secure enough to give into my exhaustion and lay down on a bench in the station, holding on tightly to my only piece of luggage, and fell asleep.

When I opened my eyes it was dawn. I stepped outside the empty terminal to see people milling around. It seemed that everyone here knew where my uncle, Jacob-the-barber, resided.

In my golden shoes, with their flapping soles and worn leather heels, I began my walk, the longest mile toward my new life: Obchod, population eight thousand. From the description of the people at the terminal, I recognized the small house where Eva and Jacob lived. The door opened before I could knock.

"Rodinkah," my aunt cried, "you are here… you're here!"

"Yacheleh, Yashinkeh," I screamed when I saw their faces.

"Oh, God, mein kindele," they said in one voice, "you're here." They chanted this like a prayer over and over.

Joined by Rachel and Ben, we reminisced about the past, grieving together and swaying back and forth in each others arms. There were tears, and laughter, and endless stories. I was loved again and I loved back. When we calmed down, they gave a good look at me for the first time.

"Rodinkah, you're so thin, so pale." My aunt put her hand on my forehead as my mother would have done and brushed it with a soft kiss.

"We're going to stuff you with potatoes and bread until the pink comes back into your cheeks."

I was home and could collapse into the security of my aunt's arms. I was weak, so I slept until my aunt would wake me up with a meal. It took me the entire winter to regain my strength. Even though potatoes were our main dish, the little edibles we had here was much better than what I ate in Cheboksary. My aunt also supplemented our poor bread ration from the store with her own delicious baked bread. But the bread alone was never enough. Occasionally, we had peas, oat bran, cabbage, beets, onions and garlic. It would become a great sensation when my uncle could get lamb. My aunt would add a half pound of the lamb to the big pot of potatoes and push it deep into the upright oven for many hours to cook. Even after fifty years, I still remember the smell and taste of that delicious stew.

In the summer, we went into the deep woods and found wild raspberry bushes. We ate the berries on the spot until we became purple. The rest we brought home to dry for the winter to be used later as a cold medicine.

The winter was endless.

It was my first winter I did not worry about warm clothing because I didn't leave the house. Since I slept most of the time, the only issue we made about clothing was who would wear what because everyone shared the few pieces that we did have. We shared the valenki and a brown woolen shawl to go to the well for water, and to the outhouse. Running home from the bitter cold, we would climb up onto the oven: the white lofty "Russkaya pechka" that was built into the tiny kitchen. It was much like a bakery oven of old, almost as high as the ceiling, and built into the wall. In the back of the oven was a cubby that could only be reached with a ladder. We would kick off our valenki, throw off our shawl and scramble up the ladder to sit in our warm cubby which heated our backsides until we could take no more: a warmth we carried away with us to remember in the cold.

The first signs of spring brought some strength to my body and relief to my mind. At that time we had begun to hear news about a few friends and relatives who had escaped from the Nazis: the Buguruslan Information Center kept records of the evacuees that helped families to reunite.

My uncle's niece, Hanna, found our address from this center and wrote to us. Hanna was Jacob's oldest brother's only daughter. Everyone in the family was relieved that she had escaped. There was no doubt in my mind that my relatives would bring Hanna to live with us. And so they did. Again we rejoiced; this time in the reunion with Hanna whom I had never met before, but here in Obchod I would share my bed with her.

In the tiny house one room was occupied by Ekaterina Malykova. She gave us the other room in which the five of us nestled. There should have been six, but Rachel lived and worked eight kilometers away in an orphanage that housed children who had been evacuated from Leningrad. Even though she visited us only occasionally for there was no transportation and it was a long dark road through the woods, she still was a strong part of the family's brain.

Since Aunt Eva did not sleep well, she would blame her sleepless nights on her husband, she shouted at him all night.

"Jacob, you start snoring even before you put your head on the pillow."

"I can hear everything that is going on," he shouted back.

"Then tell me, my dear Jacob, how many times did I get up tonight?"

He shrugged his shoulders and grinned. "You were so quiet."

While this nightly talk went on, Hanna and I, who were supposed to be asleep on the opposite side of the tiny room, had to stick our faces in the pillow to keep from laughing out loud.

"Look, Jacob, even the girls are laughing at you."

"No, they are laughing at you, Eva," he argued back.

I wished I could have stopped laughing, but it was too funny.

Then Ben would shout from the third bed: "Could you all be quiet. I have to get up early." In the evening, everyone returned home from work; we all squeezed around the small kitchen table in the corner and waited for Eva to get the big pot with hot delicious potatoes from the upright oven, anticipating indescribable moments of delight.

Hanna was a pessimist--I was her foil. Even though I still considered Tanya to be my best friend, Hanna vied for second place. While Tanya used to be fun, happy-go-lucky, fashionable, Hanna was a serious intellectual whose company I longed. We would talk for hours at a time about our childhood experiences, about books, human relations, and her romances. It was Hanna who satisfied my thirst for knowledge. She was my teacher. I was seventeen; she was twenty-four. That was in 1943. It should be understood that I admired her for her maturity, her exuberance, I loved the flash in her blue eyes when she spoke about the world. And even though she was only five feet tall, she seemed a giant in my eyes. Fifty years later she is even taller.

Obchod was known only because the railroad passed through it, and for the trees in the rich forests that were used to fuel the trains. A tiny town that never saw a Jew, nor had a church - so anti-Semitism was not an issue. People were kind to each other, and shared their poor banquet. The cold, dry winters lasted for six months. The only means of transportation was horse-drawn wagons that brought the chopped wood to the railroad. Later they built a road made of split trees wide enough for a truck to go through. But if a piece of the road slipped out, the truck would topple over. In this world, I think, there are no worse obscenities than the Russian ones--and the wagoneers and the few truck drivers used them generously like salt on a potato, even though there was a shortage of salt. This was Obchod.

This woodchopper's village had two streets, one elementary school, one store, and a diner. There was a social hall where we could watch an occasional movie or dance on Saturday night, even though the only music we had was from a harmonica and a chorus of discordant voices. It was here that Hanna met Josef.

In 1939, under Hitler and Stalin's secret agreement, Josef's little Polish town of Stry near the city of Lvov, had been taken over by the Russians. In 1941, when the war broke out between Germany and the Soviet Union, Josef was called into the Red Army to the front line. Later on, as the Russians came to mistrust the Polish Army units, they took them off the battle fields forming Polish labor battalions instead. Josef was one of the young Polish laborers forced to chop woods in Obchod. This way, his life was saved.

Like Hanna, he was short in stature, but tall in demeanor, and as quick as an otter in the way he moved. Above all, Josef was an honest man with a good soul who came to love Hanna deeply. They dated for two years, but Hanna was undecided about just how far she would let their friendship go.

After Latvia was liberated from the Nazis and Hanna and I were about to return to Riga, she decided to marry Josef, otherwise he would not be permitted to enter Riga later.

One April morning in 1945, they went to register their marriage in the town hall, four kilometers away from our village. I figured out how long it would take them to get back, and went to the well to fill up my two pails with fresh water. I did not have anything to give them as a wedding present. When I saw them at a distance, I hooked up my pails to a wooden yoke and went to greet them in the tradition of Obchod: with pails full of luck. That evening Josef was invited to share our dinner of potatoes and bread. We finished the festive meal with:

Dream Tea:

A   bowl   of
brewed dry raspberry tea

Without the golden honey of our memories.

A dash of humor and a cup of hope.

There was no place for the newlyweds to spend their first night, so Josef went back to his barracks.

My Father

I continued inquiring about my father and never lost hope that I would find him. It was a rainy autumn day when we answered a knock at the door. The mailman delivered a letter from my uncle's friend, Hirsh Knoch, with news of my father.

"My father is alive!"

The day became like spring with all the feelings of hope and renewal.

Hirsh wrote that he fought next to my father in the Latvian division of the Red Army. …That he had told my father about my mother's death, that I survived and was cared for by Jacob and Eva. From then on I waited.

One October morning the letter carrier stopped at our door again, and pulled out two triangles from his mail basket. I was out of my mind with excitement, when I saw my father's handwriting. I tore open the letter. He wrote:

"Dorogaya dochenka [My dear daughter],

It was very painful for me to learn that mother had died.

You went through so much pain alone as I am doing now.

I wished so desperately that we could have been together.

But a war is going on. It will be over soon, my darling child.

I am certain that we will be together again.

I was wounded in my shoulder. I am recently out of the hospital.

And even though I will have to go to fight the enemy again,

I want you to stay strong with the belief that I will be all right.

Don't worry, my child

Tseluyu krepko [I kiss you heartily,]

Tvoy lyubyashchiy Papa [Your loving Father.]

The other letter was to Eva and Jacob; my father thanked them for bringing me over to make it through the hard times. He knew they would keep me as their own child; he promised to repay them for everything they were doing for me.

From then on the letter carrier delivered the precious triangles from my father at least once a week. There were few men left in the village, most of the wood-chopping was done by women whose husbands were fighting at the front. I was working in an office in charge of time-tables and payroll for the wood choppers.

At least, once a month an unlucky woman would receive pokhoronoye that her husband or son had been killed in battle. At those times you could hear little Obchod wailing.

It was with the same suddenness that the cherished letters from my father appeared that they disappeared. My reaction was not immediate: it could merely have meant that mail was slow, or the battle was hot and there was no time for writing, or he was captured or wounded again. I did not want to think of the worst.

One morning Zinaida Nikolayevna, my boss, called me into her office.

"When did you receive your last letter from your father?" She asked me.

She did not let me even answer, as she went on:

"Milochka, [Darling] you have to go to Uren, to the County's War Affairs Department."

I understood right away that the news was bad. My fear was well founded.

"Your father had been killed."

"It can't be true, I wailed. It just can't."

I ran out of the door. I needed Aunt Eva to comfort me. She took my hand, looked at me with sad eyes.

"Maybe it's a mistake, my Rodinkah, we will find out."

The train from Siberia to Moscow stopped in Obchod at three o'clock in the morning. Seldom did people get off in our small town therefore the car doors were locked up. I had no other choice than stand on the steps of the car and hold onto the frozen door handles then carefully move to the connector between the cars, as the train gained speed.

When the train arrived, the town of Uren was in slumber, so I had to wait in the cold terminal before I could walk to the War Affairs Department. The snow was deep, but now I had my own valenki. Later, as the sun melted the snow, my woolen boots filled with slush. When I arrived, a woman behind the desk handed me a small piece of paper:

"Your father was killed defending the Motherland," she said as she handed the pochoronoye to me.

It did not say when he had been killed or the place where he had been buried.

I knew that twenty million Soviet people were killed in World War II. We mourned every dead soldier; collective grief was in all the hearts.

But this was my father, my blood, my soul. I could not contain my hot and salty tears which kept running down my cheeks mourning at the Uren terminal where I had to wait for yet another day for the train to go home. I sat in the terminal shivering with cold, hunger and grief.

When I finally arrived home everyone was waiting. Again we cried together, this time for death.

This happened in March 1943. To this day I keep the memorial of my father, in the same way as I keep my mother's "Yortzeit:" on the day when I learned of his death.

I was an orphan now, an empty soul who had to find once again a meaning in life and something to hope for. My pride would not let me accept self-pity; I had to pull myself together. To keep my mind off my grief, Uncle Jacob started to involve me in his "business" more than before. Even though there was no private business permitted in the Soviet Union, hunger does not know restraint.

My Uncle Jacob was not a barber, but rather a successful entrepreneur. Only three years before, besides being an owner of a fabric store, he was engaged in another business of buying fruit from the orchards when the trees were in early bloom. It was as if he were a commodity buyer of futures in the stock market. Jacob was a lucky gambler, but all of his businesses were nationalized by the Russians.

In 1941, when World War II broke out, Jacob grabbed his family, his barbering tools and ran from the Nazis. As a young soldier in the Czar's army in World War I, those same tools had saved him from going to the front line. They saved him again in World War II - Obchod bosses needed a barber, but not another soldier. When the shop was closed, the elite of our village came to our house for haircuts and shaves. They paid Jacob with vodka, bread coupons, and with sacks of oats which they too schemed to acquire. We accumulated these goods and then exchanged them at the marketplace for things we needed. To get a bar of soap or a glass of salt, we bartered whatever we had. In the winter we traded our goods for lamb. One could see my uncle and me each carrying on our backs sacks which were loaded with a pud of weight. In the cold winter and in the hot summer we walked six kilometers each way to the market. Uncle Jacob thought of me as his right hand, his advisor and cashier with whom he shared all the stories of his business deals. I still continued my job in the office, giving my entire salary to Jacob. I felt good to contribute to the family's welfare.

While everyone worked outside the household, Aunt Eva kept the house running. She learned from Ekaterina, our neighbor, how to make liquid soap out of ashes and water, a rich soup out of water and potatoes. She held us, our clothes, our sheets together with patches she took from other places. Even though Jacob and the children were the bread winners, without Eva the bread could not have been baked: she was the strength of the family. In addition to all of Eva's other talents, she was a physically beautiful woman with flaxen hair, a small straight nose, and clever hazel eyes which just like my grandmother's held the secrets of the universe.

Reunited With Old Friends

War brings strangers together and keeps them intact with an invisible string of common experience of hardship and joy. This was true for our family. One person's friend became everyone's friend. Every new letter brought one more survivor.

After three years of disconnection, I received a letter from Tanya. If the reader remembers, Tanya was my childhood friend. She with her parents settled in Kazan, a city on the Volga River, the capital of the Tatar Soviet Autonomous Republic. Because her father had a bleeding stomach ulcer, he was exempt from the army. Tanya was able to attend school where she made friends with local teenagers. In her second letter, Tanya sent me a small picture of herself with her girl friend Valya. My cousin Ben looked at this picture and asked me:

"Which one was Tanya?" I pointed. Then he said lightly: "Oh, the one with the turned-up nose?"

A long time had gone by before I received Tanya's third letter with sad news:

Her forty-year-old mother had been killed by a truck which took her to bring lunch for her husband. Tanya's loss opened my own unhealed wounds: I could not bear new tears and new sorrow. My Aunt Eva wrote a letter of comfort for me to Tanya.

"Dear Tanya,

... You are still young. Your wounds will heal.

You'll meet a true friend in life and be happy again."

My aunt could not know then when she wrote that letter that just in two years her son Ben would be that true friend.

****

The year was 1944. The news from the front improved as the Soviet Army regained lost territories. At this time we received the most unexpected letter. It was from Chona, Eva and Jacob's oldest son. We had given up hope that he had survived. We could find him neither through the Buguruslan Information Center, nor through other people. Instead he found us. He had escaped from Riga where he was studying mechanical engineering. He wrote that he settled in Kara-Kalpak, an Autonomous Republic within Uzbekistan, near the Iranian border. He was not in the army because of poor eye sight. Our joy was as a two sided coin: on one side there is unadulterated hope; on the other—fear when we realized that even with his poor eyes, Chona could lose his exempt army status if he came to Obchod. We finally decided that he should join us, hoping that with his father Jacob's connections he would be given an army release status here as well.

Our joyous reunion did not last too long for Chona was soon called into the war. There was nothing that his father could do for him.

CHAPTER V
RETURN TO RIGA
Unfulfilled Dreams

On October 13, 1944, Riga was liberated from the Nazis. Everyone hoped that Hitler's defeat was close. Hanna and I began to dream about returning home. It was decided that both of us go first, and the rest of the family would follow.

On April 11, 1945, we kissed Aunt Eva, Uncle Jacob, Rachel, Ben and Josef good-bye. We were returning to our birthplace, to yet another new and hopefully better life, to our Riga.

We were both young, full of hope and determination. I had two goals: first, to get a job with the food industry, so that I would have enough to eat; second, to enroll in school and continue my interrupted education. Even though Hanna was a teacher, I thought of a more practical job for her. I suggested she finds a position of an economist either in the office where the ration coupons were distributed, or where they were redeemed. We chatted away the trip.

We had finally reached our last train connection point in Daugavpils, a city already on Latvian soil. We stood in a long line to confirm our tickets, when I spotted Sarah, the young woman who had helped me find my relatives. She had returned to Riga right after the liberation, she told us. She had a job and was sent on business to Daugavpils. Hanna had nobody to go to in Riga, but I had my Uncle Yudle, the husband of my father's youngest sister, Riva.

At the onset of the war, Yudle decided that it would be safer for his wife and three children, Liana, Ben and Anri, to avoid the constant bombardments in Riga. He took them to his parents home in a distant province of Vilyaki, near the Russian border. Yudle himself returned to Riga to defend the city. He fought in the Red Guard together with my father. Events in Riga developed rapidly as the Germans moved swiftly into the city. All roads were cut off and Yudle could not return to his family in Vilyaki. Neither could they escape from the Nazis.

Now, coming back to Latvia, after having been seriously wounded in the war, he rushed to his home town where he left his family to discover that they had been murdered by the fascists. Broken by this unbelievable tragedy, he returned to Riga. Yudle could not bring himself to enter the apartment where he so happily used to live, and decided to go see what happened to my apartment. He learned that the maintenance woman in charge of the building moved to our apartment right after the Germans had occupied Riga. On the day of the Russian liberation, she moved out to a different neighborhood taking all of our possessions with her. During Yudle's visit to my apartment a soldier appeared. This was Chona. The two men embraced each other, they thought they both survived the war. Even though the major part of Latvian territory had been liberated, the German army still entrenched themselves beyond Riga in the direction toward the shores of the Baltic Sea. Chona was ordered to return to his unit. Shortly before the victory, he was killed in battle for the Latvian town of Jelgava.

In his letter Yudle invited us to stay with him when we return to Riga. On the train, on our way home, Sarah told me that she knew he had remarried. Yudle himself did not mention this to me.

Now accompanied by Sarah, Hanna and I arrived at sunset. The city looked strange to me. I did not see familiar faces. Sarah's apartment was cold. Riga lacked fuel, water and electrical power, so she used books that were left by the Nazi followers to heat the place.

When the chill was out of the air, she began to talk.

"All the Jews in Riga were massacred by the Nazis and the Latvian fascists. The murderers are still alive. They fled the liberated Latvia together with those who did not support the communists' ideas. All of them were placed in relocation camps in Germany waiting for affidavits from family and strangers in North America, Canada, Latin America and Australia."

I could not bear the pain of what the Germans had done to my grandmother Malka, to my aunts, uncles and cousins, to my friends, to my teachers.

We learned, as did the world, that the Jews could have been saved, had there been external help. Instead, the civilized world blocked out information that came to them about the ghettos, about the concentration camps, about the gas chambers.

We talked all night. At dawn I rushed to see my Uncle Yudle, the only person here with whom my childhood was threaded. I longed to put my head on his shoulder and together cry out our mourning.

An older woman opened Yudle's apartment door. Fanya Borisovna was Yudle's new mother-in-law. She guessed that I was the niece who returned home.

"I am insulted that you stayed with a friend, she scolded, you have to move in here immediately, otherwise Yudle will be hurt. He is out of town but will return tonight."

There was already a room prepared for Hanna and me. I would not disappoint him;

how could I ignore his sincere hospitality? Later, when Eva, Jacob and the children arrived, they too found a shelter in Yudle's home.

We moved in and settled quickly before his wife Fira arrived from work; together we were waiting for Yudle. His new family made us feel at home; however, my heart was crying silently for the loss of my Aunt Riva and the children, but I gave no indication of my feelings.

On May 9, 1945, as we were sitting at the breakfast table and enjoying omelets cooked out of American egg powder, we suddenly heard noise coming from the street. We looked out the window: the street was crowded with people.

We left our breakfast unfinished and ran outside. Everyone was screaming:

"Victory!" Victory! The Germans had capitulated!"

We had waited for four years; finally, the Day arrived. Bands played, people danced in the streets, we sang songs. But the pain did not go away.

We, the dancers, we the singers had lost our precious loved ones and humanity as we knew it. A stranger greeted me in Vermanya park. "I too am a survivor," he said. Then he asked me a question: "what is missing in this park?" But it was he who answered his own sad question. "The laughter of Jewish children. The Nazis murdered one and a half million innocent Jewish children."

52

As painful as it was, life went on. Never having enough to eat during the war, my instincts led me to seek employment in the food industry where I found a job with "Riga Trust of Restaurants and Cafes." Because of my mathematical abilities, I was appointed to bookkeeping. There was nobody available to train me, I had to figure out the job by myself. I would be responsible for calculating the ingredients for daily menus, keep inventory of the ration coupons and redeem them on a daily basis. The calculations of the food required great accuracy for the frequent audits from the Trust itself and for the arrests by the Internal Security Department. But we, the employees, were hungry; our meager salaries could not provide even for the bare essentials.

The chef was an experienced middle-aged woman; she managed the kitchen well and still knew how to save some food for the employees. She would give me a loaf of bread or a kilogram of sugar or butter to take home. I took it even though I knew it was illegal. Everyone lived in fear: not only from the militia but also of what a neighbor would see on your table.

Ilja's Life Story

I was standing in line to redeem the ration coupons, when I noticed a familiar man in that same line. He looked like Ilja Raikin, my mother's cousin. I still could not be sure because this person seemed too old with flesh hanging on his sallow face. Still I could not let him go.

"Excuse me," I said. "Are you Ilja Raikin?"

"Yes," he answered.

He didn't recognize me either. I had to tell him who I was.

"I am a survivor of the Riga ghetto," he said, "I have already lived for a thousand years…"

After work we walked along the streets and through the parks together. As we walked, he talked.

"I was chased out of my home, and along with other Jews driven like a herd of animals, into the ghetto. Besides our valuables, the Germans didn't let us take much along. Together with their Latvian collaborators, they brought us to the worst neighborhood and fenced it off so we would not be able to get out. The conditions inside were horrible, but we adjusted.

Remember Zhenya, Uncle David's daughter?"

"Yes." I nodded.

"She went insane."

I shook my head back and forth to the rhythm of his horrible tale.

He went on, "the guards would laugh at her and tease her but I could only watch helplessly. Our tragedy became greater each day until it reached its peak. The massive Jewish execution began. I witnessed the murderers as they seized Jewish valuables. I watched as they shaved off Jewish hair, I saw them pull out Jewish gold teeth, I heard Jews screaming in death-agony… The world knows now the atrocities of the ghettos.

We were the only ones who did not know. But we learned first hand."

I was in disbelief and dizzy with hysteria, but he continued.

"It was not enough for the murderers to kill just Latvians Jews. They transported Jews from Germany, Austria and Czechoslovakia to Riga. The Rumbuli and Bikernieki forests were soaked with tears and blood. Kaiserwald and Salaspils camps cracked with human bones. But the world was silent." Ilja paused.

"What happened to the Great Choral Shuhl?" I asked, as we continued walking through parks fully blossoming with myriad of color, birds, butterflies.

"Ah," he sighed. "Such a tragedy; hundreds of people were thrown by the Nazis into this beautiful synagogue, where the world famous cantors like Moshe Kusovitsky and Herman Yadlovker, came for the High Holidays. The murderers burned it down together with the Jews."

I learned then that Zvi Gram, my Hamora school principal, my beloved mathematics teacher, was among the victims. My heart was crushed to see a square on the grounds of the Choral Shuhl: I watched parents bring their children there. No one remembered this sacred place as no one knew that the flowers grown out of the soil were nurtured with human blood and human ashes.

"Now I will tell you my personal story," Ilja said. "One night, long before the war started, I went to the movies. A pretty young woman sat next to me. After the movie was over, I started a conversation with her and invited her to the elegant "Otto Schwartz" cafe.

We saw each other frequently thereafter. One thing lead to another and she became pregnant. I didn't know what to do. I knew that I could not marry her because she was not Jewish. Our daughter Lidia was born. I supported them financially. It was meant to be that I was not with them when the Germans invaded, otherwise we all would have been killed.

My family knew that I was driven to the ghetto, so day and night they searched for me. Finally, they found me when a group of Jews was being escorted to work under close guard. The mother of my child was so brave that she bribed a guard to let her put a piece of bread into my hand. Encouraged by her success, she worked out a plan with that same guard. In exchange she slipped him gold coins. This was their plan: a trash man would hide me in the garbage in the back of his wagon, and drive me out of the ghetto to a safe place where I could remain until dark. When night approached, I walked the back-roads until I came to my family's place."

Ilja's eyes filled with tears. He paused and then continued. "They found another place for me to hide, but you can't imagine how dangerous this was for them. There have been constant raids on Jews and deserters by the Nazis. By great miracle we all survived."

Ilja invited me to meet his family. He was about to become a grandfather: his daughter Lidia was expecting a child.

Life regenerated.

CHAPTER VI

1945: THE SUMMER OF MY LOVE

Pinya and Rhoda

The hot air cooled off with summer rain. I loved the smell of the fresh clean air. I loved Riga and Riga loved me back. I had a good job, and soon I would continue my long-awaited education.

I had no dreams of a prince on a white horse yet, who had time for this fantasy, but he came anyway, and wove himself inextricably into my life.

It happened this way: one day, I returned home from work when unexpectedly I ran into Ami; the same Ami whom I met two years ago at the marketplace in a town called Shachunya. Jacob sent Hanna and me to sell a loaf of bread there. Ami's heavy Russian accent indicated to us that she was an evacuee from the Baltics. When we approached her she told us that she was from Latvia indeed. She immediately invited us to her home where we met her childhood friend Shayna with her little daughter Sima. Shayna had a great job of selling bread. Could anyone imagine what it meant to be a bread queen in the war time? We stayed with them until two o'clock in the morning waiting for our train to take us back to Obchod. Jacob liked the good news about our trip. So, from then on he would send Hanna and me to Shayna in Shachunya to redeem the extra bread coupons whenever he would get it for his barber work.

Ami and Shayna with her cute daughter had just returned to Riga from evacuation, they stayed a block away from us with a cousin of Shayna's. Ami suggested that we celebrate Jani, a Latvian summer holiday when people go to the parks to dance all night to the music of brass bands, together. By that time, Eva, Jacob, Rachel and Ben had already returned from Russia. Rachel and I accepted the invitation. The following day we came to join them. I hardly paid attention to a pimpled face young man, so skinny that his clothes hung on him, but he accompanied our crowd anyway.

The celebration in the park was at its swing. He invited me for the first dance immediately and so he continued. He would not let anyone ask me to dance.

His name was Pinya Gurevich. He danced like Pan, and eventually he loved me obsessively. From that night on, Pinya followed me everywhere; I would find him on the street waiting for me after work; I would see him walking back and forth after school at night. Pinya would watch over me like a mother watches over her child, and even though I had no thought of marriage—I had so much to do first—I needed this love.

The golden fall replaced the hot 1945 summer. The new harvest was rich that year: apples, pears and amber color plums filled Riga's Farmers' Market. There was a handful of Rigan survivors left only, they trickled home from evacuation; the air was filled with renewal.

I was rushing through Suvorova Street, when suddenly Tanya, my dear childhood friend, with her father appeared before me. They had returned from Russia that very day.

"Come with me," I exclaimed as I hugged her. "I will take you to my aunt's family." The moment we entered the house, Eva recognized her from the picture she had sent me. We all sat down at the dinner table. The hospitality in me arranged for Tanya to sit next to Ben.

Traditionally, after the meal, we remained sitting around the table: telling stories and singing. At that time the Russian war songs were popular. We sang "Solovyi," composed by the famous Solovyev-

Sedoy, a song which reflected the thoughts of a soldier resting in the woods after the battle; recollecting the spring when the nightingales sang for him and his beloved.

"Just let the war be over and we both will listen to the nightingales again."

In another song, "Lina," a soldier, sends a letter to his beloved to wait for him until he returns home from the war. If he is killed, she should not mourn. Instead, he asks her to give her love to another soldier who will survive the war.

I loved Ben's beautiful baritone voice. When Tanya joined in, we stopped singing and let them both sing together. This atmosphere created a harmony between them that would follow into a melodic future.

As Eva brings a large bowl of delicious Latvian fruit to the table, Pinya says quietly.

"It is my birthday today. I am twenty one, and also two years old."

We wish him a happy birthday. We all look at each other and roll our eyes.

"What do you mean?" We ask.

Pinya takes a deep breath, opens his mouth widely, and says:

"Come closer and look into my jaw. Can you see a hole? "

"Yes," we all say.

"Now look at my foot. It does not flex."

"No," we all say.

"This happened on my nineteenth birthday. I went to the battle and asked myself if I would live to be nineteen? The enemy was strong. It was a hard fight. Our soldiers felled like wheat with a scythe. You could hardly lift your head. But we were ordered into battle. I heard a shell explode next to my face, I felt something warm on my cheek. Blood. Still I fought on. Then something hit my foot; I lost consciousness. Next, I was in a hospital, shot near my temple. The shrapnel from the exploded mine went through my cheek and lower gum, knocking out my lower teeth. The shell-splinter came out through my chin. I was lucky then. Also, my wounded foot ached terribly. All this happened at sunset of my nineteenth birthday."

Pinya continues: "My sister who is ten years older than I, told me that I was also born on sunset. She said that my father together with her and my brother Ruven were sitting in a "Sukkah" celebrating the fall festivals when an aunt rushed in with the good news that Chava had delivered a son."

Jacob refills the glasses with wine. We toast to Pinya's twenty first birthday; to his second birthday and to Sukkot.

Pinya stands up. We are filled with the joy of survival, with joy of the wine.He raises his glass.

"I predict that Tanya and Ben will marry. Rachel and her boyfriend Boris will marry. He continuous in his firm voice, I also predict that Rodinkah will marry me."

"Sit down already," we yell in unison and laughter together.

All of Pinya's predictions came true.

****

It was one of the hardest decisions I had to make. When I was still a child, my parents would discuss my university education, my desire of learning became a part of me. On one hand, I did not want to compromise my plans for anyone or anything; on the other hand, I lived in a vacuum. I missed the love of my parents. I missed love. So I gave in.

Boris proposed to Rachel, Pinya proposed to me. Our family decided that the two couples could get married on the same day. Aunt Eva and Uncle Jacob started planning the wedding for their daughter and for me. I did not have a wedding gown and I could not afford to buy one. We made a compromise that I should wear my graduation dress which my mother had thrown into our suitcase when we fled from Hitler. The dress was made from navy blue silk and decorated with plisse edged in white silk. I did not sell it for a loaf of bread. I had not worn it during the four war years in Russia either. I brought this dress back home. But I had no shoes except for the only pair I wore every day. So Pinya came up with an idea to sell a quarter of a pound saccharin on the black market. I could buy the saccharin at a nominal price in the cafeteria where I worked. We sold the saccharin and received the money, when all of a sudden a big man caught Pinya's arm. He was an undercover militia agent who ordered us to follow him to the headquarters. He was going to file a case of speculation which would put us in jail for seven years. Fortunately, Pinya's military overcoat saved us.

He pleaded to the a militia agent who had also fought in the war, "I'm going to get married in two weeks, but my bride has no shoes for the wedding. Please, let us go."

Surprisingly, the agent's heart softened, and he let us go with a warning never again to engage in profiteering. We bought the shoes and a veil. At Eva's request, Jacob was occupied with obtaining food for the traditional Jewish meal.

Finally, the wedding day arrived. We brought the only Rabbi in town along with the huppa and the huppa poles, all driven in a horse cab to our home. We invited the best Jewish violinist, Gerson Fomin, to play the traditional wedding music. Since all religious ceremonies had been forbidden, we had to be cautious in selecting the guests to be present at the huppa. We, the brides, as well as the grooms fasted for twenty four hours as decreed by Talmudic law. Rachel and Boris' ceremony was first, ours was performed half an hour later in the other room.

All morning of that cold winter wedding day, a chilling question haunted me: why could my parents not have lived to see this day and bring me to the wedding canopy. Pinya was obsessed with the same question about his murdered parents.

Now, is the time for the ceremony: I walk into the room, the guests stand around the huppa holding lit candles in their hands. Fomin's violin cries out the melodic fragile lament of the Jewish people. I circle around the groom seven times in the tradition of my faithfulness and continuity of Judaism. The Rabbi reads the "ketuba" in Hebrew. He then recites the prayers. With a sip of wine from the silver goblet Pinya breaks the fast, I follow him. A glass wrapped in a linen cloth is set down on the floor. Up comes Pinya's foot. With a thrust of a hundred thirty pounds, he brings it down over the napkin.

"Crash!" The glass smashes into a thousand tiny shards, two thousand years remembrance of the destruction of the first Temple in Jerusalem.

"Mazal Tov!   Mazal Tov!" Everyone offers in unison. The violin plays joyous music. All dance.

Pinya holds me in his strong arms and kisses me continuously.

****

Tayglach:

(A Jewish desert for a wedding)   Dough:

6 large eggs

2 tablespoons sugar

1 tablespoon oil

Combine the ingredients

Two cups flour and 2 teaspoons baking soda.

Add more flour if needed:

Dough should be semi-firm.

Cut the strings of the dough into 4 inch pieces.
Between the palms of your hands: one at a time.

Tie into bows and let rise for 20 minutes.

Makes thirty six tayglach.

Combine in a large stainless steel pot

1 pound of honey

1 pound of sugar

2 large glasses of cold water

Stir to boiling point.

Then drop each taygle into the pot.

Set the heat on medium and cover the

Pot tightly for forty minutes.

Lift the cover slowly and stir the

Tayglach with a wooden spoon.

Add a pinch of ginger and stir very carefully.

Cover again and cook for twenty more minutes

Checking a few times.

The tayglach should be golden brown when ready.

Wet a wooden board with cold water.

Take the hot tayglach out one at a time with two spoons.

Optional: Roll in poppy seeds, coconuts or crushed nuts.

Serve in a crystal footed vase.

White linen napkin swans float on a lake of china, crystal, silver and newly starched table cloths. Silver candelabras, flowers, wines and liqueurs in sparkling decanters bring more to the festivity. Eva will not trust even a cook to handle the weddings, so she hires one to help her. Gefilte fish from the freshest Latvian whitefish is cooked early in the morning, each piece decorated with a slice of cooked carrots and arranged on long narrow platters, home made horse radish is prepared to accompany it; chopped herring served on smaller oval platters; "pucha" decorated with slices of hard boiled eggs and served on wider oval platters, accompanied by home made mustard; wide slices of juicy pickled beef briskets and tongues laid out on the same style platters as the pucha; chopped liver decorated with finely diced eggs is arranged on smaller oval platters—and on and on… like a cornucopia, Eva's food spreads itself on the table unendingly. Here comes the steaming chicken bullion in special cups and Eva's baked delicious meat piroshki to be eaten with the bullion. Roasted chicken with tzimmes and rice for the main course follow. A compote of dried fruit concludes the festive meal.

Striking toasts and speeches were offered. Finally, Eva sat down, eyes wet with tears. We danced to the music of Fomin's violin and to Zhorzhik's accordion.

The tables were set again, now laid with the traditional Jewish sweets: fluffy yellow sponge cakes contrasted with the snow-white linen tablecloths, pieces of richly golden honey cake was witness to Eva's cooking excellence, and finally, her specialty, the round honeyed tayglach the color of dark Latvian Amber, served in tall footed vases.

Thus the wedding feast came to an end.

****

I put my hand in Pinya's. We did not think of what lay ahead of us. We did not know then how bumpy our road would be. We only knew that we were walking hand in hand.

AMBERSHORE

Riga, Latvia 1946-1950

Once again Russian paranoia manifested itself when the new government brought into Latvia an endless number of Russian settlers from all over the Soviet Union, a warning that would demonstrate the strength of the regime to the Latvians. Needless to say that a shortage in housing developed. As the daughter of a deceased soldier I had priority to get my apartment back. Still I could not accomplish anything by myself. I was a teenager with no clout. It became a struggle for me to reclaim my old apartment, the apartment of my parents, the apartment in which I had spent my happy childhood years. It was not until Pinya himself, a war veteran, forced the bureaucrats into action. Finally, the apartment was returned to me. It was very sad to come home without my parents. So, here we were again, under the same roof: Aunt Eva, Uncle Jacob, Rachel, Ben and I. Soon there would be two more precious people: my Pinya and Rachel's Boris. Pinya and I remained there only for the next eight months, because I had made a commitment to leave this apartment to my aunt and uncle. How else could I fulfill my father's promise to repay them for the good they had done for me? Little was I to know then of the consequences I would encounter later. Pinya and I were optimistic newlyweds and believed somehow to come up with money to buy a place on the black market for ourselves. It is impossible to estimate the dollar amount we had to pay. It was a hardship for us and all we could accomplish was a single room in a ten room apartment which housed six other families. Our struggle continued for the next thirty one year until we finally immigrated in 1976.

In 1945, we were young, energetic and enthusiastic. The war was over, we enjoyed peace. We did not think about the future; we simply followed the stream.

Of course, the victory over fascism has been widely celebrated. The army was given noble treatment. Officers shopped in specialty stores where the goods were better than for the rest of the population; army hospitals and medical facilities provided the best physicians and medicine. So it was with entertainment. Not only the best acting companies from all over the Soviet Union came to perform in the officer's club which in the past belonged to the Latvian nationalists, here was also the best dancing. The club was like a palace; there were elegant banquet halls on each of the three floors: the Golden Hall, the Sky-Blue Hall and the White Hall. Heavy crystal chandeliers hung from the high ceilings; large windows splashed sunlight and moonlight across the glossy parquet floors. On weekends, a jazz and brass orchestra would play dance music past midnight. Pinya and I together with our friends were regulars on these dance floors.

On May 9,1946, a half year after our marriage, Riga observed the first anniversary of the victory over German fascism. Of course, we would celebrate at the officer's club. I walked over in the morning to see what the program was.

There before me on the playbill read: "Arkady Raikin."

My legendary cousin. The comedian grandson of Uncle David. I did not waste a second. I rushed into the club. The foyer was empty. I ran to the cloak room where hundreds of coats hung. A woman stood behind the counter.

"Where can I find Arkady Raikin?" I asked.

My expression, probably, told her that I would not give up if I did not get an immediate answer.

"Go, my dear, to the administrator," she said, pointing to a door. When I told him that Arkady was my relative, the administrator gave me the stage telephone number.

"Hurry," he yelled, "the matinee starts in five minutes."

With shaking fingers, I turned the three digits on the telephone. What would I say to this great legend, to this stranger? Then a quiet masculine voice cut through my apprehension.

"Hello?"

"You don't know me by name," I said on the phone, "but we are cousins."

"Maybe you're mistaken." He answered softly. "We're all looking for relatives."

"I'm not mistaken." I said, feeling a possible moment lost. "Was David Raikin your grandfather?"

"Yes," he exclaimed, a tremor in his voice. "Could you meet me after the show? I'm on in five minutes."

" I'll look forward to it," I answered in relief. In reality, I was out of my mind from excitement.

It was hard to believe at what speed I ran back home. When Eva opened the door, my expression gave away my emotions.

"We will be having company for dinner," I shouted. "Arkady Raikin is coming."

"What are you talking about?" She said mirroring my excitement. For a minute she did not believe me. Then her voice became animated also.

"Arkady Raikin? Arkady Raikin." She threw her hands up. "Where shall I start?" She ran into the pantry, opened and slammed shut the doors.

"I have to run to the farmers' market. We're having a party. Raikin, Raikin, the famous Raikin...I can't believe it."

She had enough food in the house for the Victory celebration, but she didn't have enough for Raikin. I could not go with her. I had to run in the other direction to get vodka. I had a friend who had a friend … who could get it on the black market. Within two hours Eva had her gourmet meal ready.

I barely had time to make it back to the theater. The show was over but the actors had not left yet.

It is here that I must explain that Arkady Raikin was as famous a personality to the Russian people as Bob Hope is to the American people.

From the back of the grand hall, the actors ambled down the stairs. I walked a few steps toward them, and without hesitation I went over to Arkady. I recognized him by his great presence.

"I am the one who called you." I said shyly. "Your grandfather David Raikin was the cousin of my grandfather Solomon Raikin." Arkady took my hand. I was not surprised when upon our first encounter he said to me:

"I was born in Riga."

"I had already known this from my Uncle Marcus's stories," I said.

"Marcus? Is he still alive?" I told him the story then he said. "I still remember that my parents would take me to the Esplanade for concerts. I was five then. I also remember my grandfathers house," he said.

"I'd like you to join us for dinner at our house." I invited. Much to my delight he accepted without a moment of hesitation. Then he introduced me to his wife, Roma who was a beautiful brunette. She was an actress in the company as well. Arkady excused himself to the other actors.

"Roma and I are having dinner with my newly found family."

"Go. Go." They responded happy for his good fortune.

Arkady gave me his arm. We stepped outside to find a horse and buggy, and I gave the cab driver the route so we could pass the house where the great comedian had been born. He settled in the carriage as if in the arms of his mother. He recognized the big gray stone building on the corner of Dzirnavu and Kurmanova Streets. But it would not be until seventeen years later that he had the desire to go into the apartment. Then he asked me to accompany him.

Everyone waited at home. In the beginning the atmosphere was stilted. We were shy and awestricken at having this famous person in our small home. Eva's delicious gefilte fish, chopped liver, roasted veal brisket with the Russian vodka did wonders to loosen us all up. I talked about the Raikins who were murdered in Riga. Arkady and Roma talked about the Raikins who survived the war. I could hardly anticipate another surprise, but it came when Arkady told me about Mira, a Leningrader cousin of my mother's, who resided in Riga.

Arkady invited all of us to the theater that night. This time we needed more than one horse cab to drive. Through the grace of God there were now eleven of us. Pinya was by my side. When we arrived, Roma went straight to the administrator who arranged comfortable seats for all of us, otherwise it would have been impossible to be at Arkady's show for it was a sell-out, as were all his concerts.

The hall radiated excitement, the lights went off. Instantly the elegant smiling Arkady appeared spurting on stage; the audience gave him a long standing ovation. Arkady looked as if he had become a different person from the one who sat at the table with us only an hour ago. He lightened up: the theater had been his life, he cared little about anything else. Stylistically he was a master of disguise, a satirist in whom one found laughter as well as tears. He could change from one character to another in a matter of seconds, presenting through them the horror of Soviet society, the tragedies of human weakness. Arkady's audiences were receptive to his strong messages from the stage.

Arkady carried the style and elegance of royalty, as time went on and he grew older, he began to spend summers at Ambershore, always at a prestigious resort, with special privileges provided by the Latvian government. Pinya and I visited him occasionally; most often we sent our daughters to spend a day with this man who was always surrounded by other famous actors, writers and composers. Arkady would take our daughters to the symphony concerts. The girls got a great deal of attention there, and would return home excited and enriched after spending time with the brilliant Raikin.

Too quickly the summers came to their ends. Our daughters went back to school.

Arkady was finally given government permission to take his show to London where he was sponsored by the British Broadcasting Corporation (BBC). The Englishmen loved Arkady's concerts, his professional style and his British-like demeanor and thought him to be a wealthy man, not understanding that all the proceeds from his concerts would have to be given to the Soviet government.

Through the years, Arkady got into much trouble with the government for using his talents to criticize a society dominated by dictatorship. However, the Soviets could not stop him because he had become a legend.

Soon after London, Arkady brought his show back to Riga. Again, we invited him and Roma, and now his younger brother Maxim who also became an actor in the same theater. We also invited Ilja Raikin, the cousin who survived the ghetto. Our family, like a burnt down forest had begun once again to regenerate sprouts on the tree. However, this would be our last visit with Arkady in Riga.

The next time we saw each other was twenty four years later, in New York City, where he along with his son Konstantin and daughter Katya performed at the Town Hall. Again the hall was overcrowded, this time with immigrants from the Soviet Union who came overdressed in their elegant outfits, holding flowers in their hands for Arkady. Everyone came to pay respect to the once most famous comedian. Arkady was already very ill with a heart condition. We felt lucky to see him once more, when on their tour to Boston they came to Worcester unexpectedly to spend Rosh Hashanah with our family.

Arkady performed for nearly fifty years. He died from a massive coronary disease on December of 1987, in Moscow at the age of seventy-six. To this day Arkady's theater is survived by his son Konstantin Raikin.

The day after I met Arkady, I rushed out to meet my mother's cousin Mira. A middle age woman opened the door. She looked like a queen, a person whom you would never forget after having seen her once. Her mannerliness, her speech and beauty shocked me. I found a strong resemblance to my mother, that quality unique in the Raikin family, a certain regal sensuous and mysterious beauty. We were both in excited disbelief. The Raikin garden was flowering once more.

Mira moved from Leningrad because her husband, Semyon Romanovich, a colonel, was sent to teach engineering disciplines in an Air-Force Academy in Riga. Their younger son, Alexander, served in the navy; but their older son, Boris, was killed in the war. Mira and I immediately developed a mother-daughter relationship. There were times that I thought my Aunt Eva was envious of our affinity, but Mira could never take Eva's place in my heart. I loved them both and needed them both.

We had a closeness with Semyon too, though Pinya would get into arguments with him about the Communist ideology. Semyon was a member of the Party, otherwise he could not have held the high position at the Academy. He fiercely believed the Party to be ideal, never accepting Pinya's viewpoint of the Soviet Union and its corrupt party system. Millions of people trusted the system, so did my cousin Alexander. However, after the fall of the Communist regime, in 1990, he wrote from Russia to me: "As sad as I am that my father is dead, I must admit that I am almost relieved that this happened before the big changes came; it would have been a great shock to my father to face discovered atrocities of the Soviet government, a government in which he believed so faithfully for a lifetime."

****

I was expecting my first baby and was concerned that our child would never know the word "grandmother" and "grandfather." Mira responded to my pain by accepting the role of the grandmother to Anechka who was born on the same date as Mira. Six years later, she together with Pinya and me were anticipating the new addition in our family. Our second child Evinka was born. Not only was I blessed with the support of Mira and Semyon, but I also benefited from their knowledge: I felt an urgent need for my intellectual fulfillment, a need to build a business career, I wanted to become a role model for our children. Semyon advised me on how to continue my education which had been interrupted by the war. Mira taught me to love the symphony; she took me to concerts and to music lectures. She provided me with literature on the lives of famous people. On our frequent visits to their home we made a habit to discuss our impressions. As Anechka and Evinka grew older, I used the same experience with them. Going together to the symphony, to the ballet and theater, reading the same books developed not only a common interest but also a close family link.

Our mutual affection with Mira and Semyon went on for thirty years. But when the time came for us to emigrate to America, needless to say, they were unhappy with our decision. For one thing, we would be far away, for another, they did not, nor did they want to understand democracy. We would be traitors to their cause.

****

Life under the Soviet regime has been like life in a jail with invisible bars. However, our understanding of the reality came to us slowly. It was not until the 1950-s, that through the eyes of my cousin Lily from Leningrad, we understood the political truth in which we lived. She warned us not to trust anyone and not to have false hopes when the Soviet government promised a bright future, lies which were told to the Soviet citizens since 1921 when Lenin introduced his "New Economic Policy" (NEP). Her parents clung to the idea of a strong economic future. After all, what was better than a free enterprise system which was what NEP was about. Could the experienced Russian businessmen anticipate the shrewdness of Lenin's plan? Small and large businesses sprung up everywhere and as a result the economy did improve greatly. The New Economic Policy was created only to revive the stagnation of the young communist country but soon after Lenin's death, Stalin was to destroy the "New Economic Policy" along with the "Nepmen" as a class whose wealth was expropriated, and the people exiled to Siberia.

Riga, Latvia 1950-1953

The Soviet propaganda machine had an enormous power over the people who trusted the government's continuous promises that life would improve after the five-year economic plans were fulfilled. We too followed like sheep. We believed that in a matter of time personal

70

income would increase; we believed that the stores would be well stocked with food and consumer goods; we believed that everyone would live happily ever after, soon. This was only a fairy tale.

The more experienced Soviet citizens began to organize small enterprises under the government umbrella; they created sources of additional income to supplement the poor economic system. Despite the strict Soviet jurisdiction rules, the human mind developed plans, most illicit. As an example, a system of manufacturing black-market goods through a chain of co-operatives arose all over the huge Soviet Union, and Latvia was no exception. There was a network of small factories, producing items such as lingerie, shirts, jerseys, dresses, rubber boots, rain-coats, food to name but a few.

The new entrepreneurs created a well-controlled business strategy and an easily coordinated accountability system. In the back alleys brief orders were given.

"I need a thousand extra pounds of yarn for jerseys."

"I will deliver the yarn in three days." Was the reply.

The factory would knit the yarn into cloth and then make two thousand jerseys which would in turn be sold for a black market profit through the co-operative retail chain as a normal transaction. After the deal was completed, the invoice would be shredded. No evidence left, no records kept.

The business men lived in constant fear of the government and of trusting the wrong people inside the organization. Government officials were just as shrewd. They found ways of putting informers into every deal. Luckily, the corrupt government bosses used the information for their personal gain accepting bribes from the co-operatives. Nevertheless, there were numerous instances when the black marketers were caught and sentenced for breaking Soviet law. After two decades of the co-operatives' existence, the government ordered to liquidate it. This action had a reverse effect when a shortage in consumer goods developed. The conventional manufacturing chain was not able to provide the needed goods because there was no incentive to work hard enough under a careless compensation system and poor material supply.

The lines in the stores became longer; the shelves emptied quickly. You could hear the disgruntled consumers grumbling in the lines. "The Jews must have been here. The shelves are bare. They bought the place out." Up the line their muttering traveled from one to another--always about the Jews. Once again the economy failed, once again the Jews were the scapegoats. Anti-Semitism was on the rise again.

****

CHAPTER VII

SOVIET REALITY

The Birthday Party

The Rigan people did not live quite by the Soviet philosophy. The Riga Jews had their own dreams. They hoped that someday the iron chains would vanish and they could go to Israel or somewhere else toward freedom.

In the meantime, we, the survivors of the horrors, tried to hold on to our own ways of life.

In the early fifties, Riga's farmers' market was still well supplied with food. Just as it was before the war, now along with our own Latvian farmers the Lithuanian farmers would bring their produce here to sell. In the winter with the holiday season starting, the huge meat pavilion did not have enough room to display their products. Special long tables were set-up outside to sell ducks, geese, turkeys and chickens. The farmers slaughtered the birds at night and sold them fresh next morning. Dear reader, rather than using the simplest term, poultry, I specifically used the names of the different birds because it was not long afterward that ducks, geese, turkeys disappeared from the market resulting from lack of grain to feed them.

People in Riga loved to gather, loved to arrange parties and would look for any occasion as a reason—the tradition intensified after the war. Tanya and I would make big birthday parties for our daughters. We shopped together at the farmers' market. We remembered again how to enjoy life. We ambled arm in arm along the tables, outside in the cold. We giggled and planned, we were only twenty-seven. Life was sweet … then it turned bitter-sweet.

In March of 1953, Tanya made plans for her six-year-old daughter Edochka's birthday party.

It happened just two months before, on January 13, 1953, that the Soviet news agency "TASS" splashed the horrible information about nine Kremlin physicians, seven of whom were Jewish. They were accused of poisoning Zhdanov who was Stalin's most likely successor.

Needless to say, the doctors were dismissed and incarcerated in small jail cells where they awaited their trials. In the big cities, this sweep of anti-Semitism was delivered to the working masses in the form of meetings where workers-communists would address the "crime," using pre-printed standard speeches prepared by the party bosses. The goal was to proclaim the doctors guilty and demand death sentences for them. This story was supposed to be followed by much greater atrocities when rumors were floating in the air that Jews could not be trusted and should be expelled to a Jewish autonomous region in Siberia, a malaria infested area, called Birobijan. The Jews did not believe this to be true until the evil news spread all over the Soviet Union. Again, Jews in Riga started packing.

Tanya had still decided to celebrate Edochka's birthday disregarding the political atmosphere. It was at the same time that Stalin became seriously ill. The radio updated his state of health hourly. Our daily worries were put to rest by the vodka and the delicious home-made food. The birthday party was in its swing when the Moscow news anchor, Levitan, in his slow but firm voice, made the astonishing announcement.

"The great Communist leader, the Generalissimo Josef Visarionovich Stalin is dead."

Everyone mourned and worried. No one could predict the consequences.

Even so, we still continued the birthday celebration with food and songs. Ben's father, my Uncle Jacob, his sharp mind always focused on the moment, cautioned us to stop singing so we would not draw attention to the apartment. "The neighbors will report us to the authorities. We will be accused of celebrating Stalin's death." The beautiful birthday child began to cry. "From now on I'll never have a birthday party." It was no wonder that this six-year-old could contemplate so maturely. She was, as were all our children, brainwashed since birth, with stories about grandfather Lenin and Stalin, both worshipped like idols. I can still hear our children singing:

Ya malenkaya devochka

[I am still a little girl, so]

Tantsuyu e poyu

[I love to sing and dance]

Ya Stalina nye videla

[I did not meet Joe Stalin yet]

No ya yevo lyublyu.

[But I love him in advance.]

****

The Murderers

This could only be possible under the Soviet dictatorship regime, that the population was held in stone-blind secret about everything. The "great leaders" were portrayed as the most reliable and capable genius to take the country into an ideal future, into communism. Nobody really knew who Josef Visarionovich Stalin was. It was not until his death that the truth about him became public knowledge. Stalin had never been in the front rows of the Bolshevik Revolution. The brilliant revolutionaries-orators like Trotsky, Zinoviev, Lunacharsky were in the vanguard. It was not until the 11th party congress, in 1922, the last congress attended by Lenin, that Stalin was appointed secretary general of the Communist Party. Being in this high position, Stalin took control of the party and through it of the government. Even though the Bolsheviks had pledged themselves to respect and secure Soviet democracy, they did not fulfill their promises. Instead, the new regime had developed a single-party system. In 1923, Stalin together with Zinoviev and Kamenev formed a triumvirate with the purpose of debarring Trotsky from power, who was regarded as Lenin's successor. In his last will, Lenin advised his followers to remove Stalin from the general secretariat of the party for his rudeness and abuse of power. But Stalin, supported by the other triumvirs, retained his position. In a constant struggle against his opponents, he abolished whatever freedom of expression still existed within the party, and transformed the party into a monolithic body. In 1925, having defeated Trotsky, Stalin broke with the other triumvirs; in 1929, he expelled Zinoviev and Kamenev from the party. Stalin went on with his bloody policy of murdering innocent people and it was through the "doctors case" that he intended to implement his anti-Semitic plans.

A secret assignment was given to the personnel departments of all companies in big cities. The same assignment was given to the housing committees: they had to prepare lists of all Jews. At that same time far away from the Metropolitan area, in Birobijan complexes of barracks were being built.

The militia along with the KGB had a special role in this comprehensive plan: it was their duty to control the preparation of the lists, so that no Jew would be left out. A funny story circulated about a prominent publisher who worked in a literature publishing house. A denunciation was received that this publisher has been missing from the Jewish lists. The publisher, born in distant kolchoz in the Urals, swore that he had been baptized.

"I'll prove it to you so you can see that I am not circumcised."

The Moscow authorities sent a written inquiry about this man to his kolchoz. The answer to Moscow stated: "we don't know what a Jew is but if it is a new breed of cows we almost have no cows in our farm left, they all died because of lack of fodder."

Nikolay Polyakov, who was appointed secretary of deportation by Stalin, wanted to get the guilt off his chest. So, before his death, he testified that the deportation of the Jews would have taken place in February of 1953. But the lists were not completed yet. Stalin, in his cruelty, set a final date of March the 5th to March the 7th of 1953, to try the doctors. The death sentences were scheduled to be announced on March 11th and on the 12th, 1953. Immediately after the trial, the Jewish population had to be deported.

A historian, Yevgeny Tarle, testified that even though the barracks were not ready, this would not create an issue, for a great part of the deported Jews would have been killed by the outraged Russian workers en route before reaching Birobijan anyway.

The plot with the doctors was the preamble to provoke the Russian workers against the Jews. Comfortable apartments of the Jewish intelligentsia, with rare art and book collections, were already assigned to be granted to the Russian officials.

It was the great miracle that none of this happened since after an extensive meeting on the Jewish liquidation, which took place all night to the early morning hours, of March 1 1953, Stalin suffered from a comprehensive stroke from which he never recovered. He died on March 5, 1953.

****

After Stalin's death, a reorganization of the Soviet Communist party and the government had been announced. Malenkov became the head of the new "triumvirate leadership." The other two were Molotov and Beria.

It became known that Lavrenty Beria had a history of torture and murder. It was no accident that Stalin summoned him to Moscow, appointing commissar of internal affairs in place of Yezhov who had been the executor of Stalin's crimes. Beria, who had shot Yezhov, retained his position longer than any of his predecessors.

Beria climbed his political ladder swiftly to become soon head of KGB, member of the Central Committee of the Communist Party and the Politburo.

Before long, Malenkov denounced Beria for his criminal anti-party and anti-state activities. Beria was executed at the end of 1953. The same year which could have become one of the bloodiest years for Jews in the Soviet Union.

The truth behind the official accusations made against Beria was that he intended to structure the KGB to become the only instrument of political power in the Soviet Union and establish his own personal dictatorship.

****

Riga, Latvia 1953-1956

It was an exciting time for me; it was a hard time too. In this political tension within the country I was studying for my graduation exams and I was pregnant. With my heavy belly, I stood in front of my professors defending my thesis in Soviet economics, statistics and accounting. I still smile when I remember my teacher, Ekaterina Tatarina, who set a precedent by allowing me to answer the examining committee's questions while sitting down.

Two weeks later, I delivered my second child.

The reader may be interested to know that not only does a Soviet husband not do breathing exercises with his wife in preparation

76

for the birth, he is not even allowed into the delivery room. And according to the Soviet sanitary rules, he cannot see the mother and his newborn child until he comes to take them home. So, seven days later, Anechka, my six year-old, with her daddy, picked me up carrying Evinka, the newest member of the Gurevich family.

Another great event happened to us before Evinka was born, we were able to make an exchange deal; we moved into two rooms of a three room apartment to share with only one family instead of six families. And to add to our luck we held two winning tickets for the Soviet Bond Lottery: one for fifty rubles; the other for twenty, a king's ransom equivalent to a month's salary which would hardly provide food for a week. Pinya wanted me to stay home, to take care of the children. However, no one knew, not even my Pinya, that I was preparing to continue my education and studied for the entrance exams secretly.

We soon understood that I had to go back to work, we simply could not make it financially. Again, I had to postpone my further education for another, more convenient time. But before I could even go back to work, I needed to find help with the children.

The harsh conditions in the Kolchoz forced many young women to flee the collective farms and move to the city. Unlike the United States in which we have freedom to live anywhere, in the Soviet Union you could remain in a city for no more than twenty-four hours without being registered with the Internal Affairs Department. The kolchoz girls figured out a way to settle in Riga: they found families who needed help, so their deal was to work for a small salary and food in order to gain the right to live in Riga. Later, these girls found employment in the factories, a place to live and quit the housekeeping jobs. I had no other choice than make these arrangements.

Her name was Nadia. As a child she and her family were forced by the Germans to move from Russia to Latvia. Long before she came to live with us, Nadia, a young girl then, was sent to work as a servant to a wealthy farmer's family. As she grew older, she fell in love with the farmer's son, Andrey. Soon Nadia's dreams were shattered when the Russian liberators exiled the wealthy Latvian farmers to Siberia. In this way Andrey's parents, brother and sister were destroyed in the gulag, only Andrey survived. After Stalin's death, he was liberated from the camp and returned to Riga. Nadia and Andrey decided to get married. Not only did Pinya and I arrange the wedding for them, we also let them share with us our two rooms until they could find housing of their own. Andrey finally got a job in a small town near

Riga, Nadia gave birth to their baby boy, but her happiness did not last for she discovered that her husband became an alcoholic. She divorced him. We had no luck with another house-keeper as she almost burned down our apartment when she left a soup cooking on the stove, the baby sleeping in the crib, dressed herself in my clothes and so careless left the house for the day. If not for neighborly intervention our tragedy could have been unfathomable.

****

Good-bye, Good Friends

It was not in our power to change our life in the Soviet Riga. This was a system rooted in lies and fraud. Everyone stole from the government in one or another way. I would not let Pinya to get involved in illegal business for I was afraid that he would be caught and jailed. What would I do without his strong support? So, I chose to work hard along with him to help make a living. And so I did for my entire life. However, some were luckier.

In 1957, a window of opportunity opened for Polish people in the Soviet Union. Our great friends Hanna and Josef were among the lucky ones. There was a renewed decree in the Soviet Union that allowed Polish citizens who lived in Poland until 1939 to return to their home-land. Josef persuaded Hanna to leave Soviet Riga and through Poland try to get to Israel. This idea inspired Tanya who was born in Vilna, Poland, to inquire about her emigration rights. And even though her parents moved to Riga when she was a baby, Tanya and her family qualified for emigration. Now both of my best friends were about to leave Riga. We were to stay here.

Tanya and Ben, Hanna and Josef were our best friends. We had celebrated our lives together: the births of our children, the death of our loved ones, birthdays and anniversaries, holidays and social occasions. We drank, we laughed, we cried together. We planned our future together. We walked the Ambershore together. And now they were leaving. My heart was broken with thoughts that I would never see them again. But the pain was not just ours. I was heartbroken for my Aunt Eva, Ben's mother. He was her sweet son. Now she would be left with only his letters about Tanya and her little granddaughter Edochka, and with the task of sending canned food to them so they could survive in their Polish life. She continued this task when after eighteen months the Frieds would move from Lodz to Vienna.

****

Ben earned his living by driving a taxi in Lodz, Poland. Within four months he suffered an automobile accident in which he fractured his back. However, he did not waste the three months he was in bed on his back. He was learning the cloth dyeing business, an industry in which he worked in Riga. He planned to bring this skills and knowledge with him to America where he had eight uncles and an aunt whom he hoped would spread their welcoming arms. But Ben could not get an American visa.

So he decided to take his family to Vienna. They boarderedd a train with a group of Jews emigrating to Israel. After a fourteen hour trip Ben, Tanya and Edochka simply walked off with the others, but walked in a opposite direction. They entered Austria illegally. With the little money they had, they rented an apartment. Interestingly, when they approached the Hebrew International Aid Society (HIAS) for help, they turned them away and almost arrested their little family. At that time the HIAS helped only refugees who were going to Israel. But Ben was determined to take his family to America. He had to find a solution fast because the police were on their trail. Through other émigrés, Ben found another more extreme solution. Others had been helped by the Catholic Diocese. However, there was a catch: they would have to convert to Christianity. Ben decided to go through the procedure just to get the visas. But when they walked through the ornately carved doors into the church and gazed at the hanging Christ illuminated by the screaming colors of stained-glass they turned away in shame and walked out. They were Jews. And like thousands of others in Jewish History they gave up their only opportunity for freedom. But our God is a forgiving God and with His help, Ben, Tanya and their daughter Eda landed on the American shores on May 21, 1959.

****

Josef and Hanna were not successful in Poland where they were kept for many months before they could first immigrate to Italy, then by boat from the Mediterranean city of Genoa finally reach the Israeli shores in 1959.

****

Nikita and Us

Until Stalin's death, the Soviet Union knew only two great Communist leaders: Lenin and Stalin. At that time, we believed everything we were told by Soviet authorities. The propaganda machine was never silent. We were continuously warned about the threat of imperialism to our peaceful life and we believed their lies. The collective government which took power after Stalin's death, was overthrown by a man little known to the people, a member of the Communist Politburo, who was supported by the majority in the Kremlin. This man became well known to the West as Nikita Sergeyevich Khrushchev.

The young Nikita was an active participant in the politics of the Bolshevik Revolution of the Ukraine. Being a party leader of the Donets mine basin he became secretary of the Communist party in Kiev. Khrushchev was soon a full member of the Politburo; one of the Supreme rulers of the Soviet Union.

On the eve of World War II, Khrushchev was in charge of the annexation of Poland's territories by USSR acquired after the secret agreement with Germany. When the Germans invaded the USSR, Khrushchev organized the evacuation of the Ukrainian industry to the east, deep into Russia. During World War II, he became known as Military Council of the Western and Southern fronts and leader of the

80

partisan warfare behind the German lines in the Ukraine. Khrushchev played an active role in the defense of Stalingrad. For all his achievements, he was given a military rank of lieutenant general. After the expulsion of German armies from Kiev at the end of 1943, he suppressed all opposition to Soviet rule and restored the region's economy.

In 1949, he was summoned to Moscow. After Stalin's death, in 1953, Khrushchev remained a member of the "collective leadership." At first he did not appear to be one of the principal contenders for the succession of Stalin. However, in the next few years he initiated many sweeping reforms in domestic and foreign policy, conflicts around which had developed between him and other leaders.

In 1956, at the 20th Party Congress of the Soviet Communist party, Khrushchev made a comprehensive denunciation of the Stalin atrocities.

Thus Khrushchev became General Secretary of the Communist Party, the leader of the Soviet Union. His power promised some changes, the most important of which was the massive liberation of the innocent political prisoners, called by Stalin "enemies of the people."

Khrushchev brought psychological relief to the people by removing certain restrictions: he unlocked a window to the West, albeit the sliver of a window. To a small degree he opened up the press promoting cultural exchange. He wanted to bring extensive agricultural reforms to the country: on one hand, he occupied himself with constant administrative reorganizations of the Soviet agricultural apparatus, on the other hand, he believed in the theories of a leading Soviet agrarian scientist, Lysenko, who perverted the scientific study of agriculture giving into political pressure. Khrushchev became fascinated by his first visit to the United states in the fall of 1959, he witnessed the dynamics of an Iowa farm belonging to Roswell Garst. For the first time, he saw corn being cultivated in the right way. From his observations, Khrushchev planned to improve Soviet crops so he could revive the declining beef and dairy industry by providing richer fodder to the livestock. In his desperate need for immediate success, he did not consider differences in weather and soil conditions. Instead of letting the soil rest and rotating fields, he rotated crops. The Soviet Union was hungry again.

****

One day there was a Russian leader named Khrushchev, the next day he disappeared. The day after we learn of a new Russian leader, Leonid Ilyich Brezhnev, another savior of the Soviet people. Nothing changed for us. We were continuously cooking in the same rancid juices.

If "Nikita" ruined the agricultural economy, what did it matter to us? The next leader was worse. With each new leader the store shelves became more empty; sausages, meat, shoes, fabric, everything one needs could not be bought. A pair of shoes would cost half of my salary. We made adjustments; we made connections; we bought things through the black market. The real leaders were the food and department store managers who held their merchandise under the counter.

My Professional Life

My job in the restaurant business kept me from hunger after the war, but there was no excitement, no fulfillment for professional potential. I looked for a more stimulating career. With the recommendation given by my Uncle Yudle, who was director of a small factory, I was hired by the marketing department with the largest factory in Riga, called "VEF," which manufactured phone switching equipment the equivalent to AT&T. The new environment, new people, new assignments stimulated my professional life, this was the place from which I would explore my creativity. Soon, I became the group manager; two years later, my big boss, Anatoly Mironov, appointed me assistant to the chief of marketing. However, my promotion did not go through since I refused to join the Communist Party. At that time Pinya was with a small knitting company, until I persuaded him to change jobs, to come to "VEF." Little was I to know that soon he would become management in a mechanical shop which employed over one hundred people. We both gave ourselves fully and honestly to our professional lives.

I felt a need to go back to school for my advanced degree in economics, but our children were still young and I wanted to spend more time with them; also Pinya objected to my plans. However, a few years later I insisted on continuing my education, I explained to Pinya that I had the evenings and one day off a week to study. Pinya argued that the children and he needed this precious time. I argued that we had everything under control: the children's school; the household. Then I'd touch his face with my hand. "I can't do this without you, my dear. It's a small commitment of time for a better life for all of us." How could he say "no?"

"OK, OK." He finally supported my decision. So I went back to school.

Our Children's Education Values

English was Anna's beloved language since fifth grade. She would come home from school very exited about her English classes. Once she told Pinya and me that she will proceed with English through the University. We both smiled knowing that she had so many years ahead to finish school; she could change her mind about her future profession. Nevertheless, Anna remained faithful to her first choice. Anna's decision prompt Pinya and me to provide English education to Evinka as well. At that same time, the Ministry of Education organized special schools with the emphasis on a foreign language such as, English, French or German. We transferred Eva to the English school. Our nine-year old Evinka was accepted after going through special tests. There was great excitement in our home, but not without worry because

Evinka would have to take the trolley and cross two busy streets each way. I was very nervous every single day until she called me at work after school.

On August 31, 1965, in the old part of the city, Pinya and I waited for our University student, Anechka, to walk with the new students and all the professors demonstrating the might of the future Latvian intellect. There she was amidst the others. Our daughter. Strength, determination and pride shone on her face, tears of happiness in mine.

Right from the beginning, Anna was a gifted linguist. French and Latin came as easily to her as did English. Later, the foreign language students worked as tour guides which afforded them opportunities to practice their English.

One day Anna waited for a ship to arrive from London. How excited she was, she told me, to watch its tiny body show up on the horizon, the small body moved closer to the shore to become a big ship, filled with tourists. She was assigned to guide them for four days through Riga. Next day she came home with news that a young man named Lionel praised her excellence in English. Anna told me of their conversation.

"How come I had not noticed you on the ship before?"

"You could not have because I was not traveling. I am only a Riga tour guide."

"But you look and sound English. So I naturally thought you were one of us"

"Unfortunately, I am not."

Anna felt confident in her knowledge, and now reinforced by Lionel's words, she had no doubt that after graduation she would be hired as a guide for English speaking tourists.

Anna sent her application to the Riga Bureau of Tourism. She did not get a response. She went to find out why did not she hear from them. They told her to come back later. Eventually the answer was "Nyet." [No.] Later Anna learned that no Jews were hired to guide foreign tourists. This was Anna's first disappointment with the Soviet system. Pinya and I were not surprised for we knew the reality of our life.

The teenage generation realized that there was no future for them in the Soviet Latvia. They also understood that excellence in studies did not mean much if you were a Jew.

That same year, Eva, graduated from high school. She decided to study econometrics at that same Latvian University, but there was competition. The University accepted new students according the results of their entrance exams. Although Eva finished a fraction below the highest score, she still qualified with five other students with similar scores. It was already August 30, two days before school would begin, but she had not heard from the University. I did not want Eva to sit home and dwell on her uncertainty, so I asked her to go with me for fruit to the farmers' market. It was a gorgeous summer morning; the nature, with its cool breeze, reminded that fall was approaching. Eva suggested that we walk instead of taking the trolley. She chose a route which would pass the University, the most beautiful area in Riga. The trees bent their heavy branches over the canal with the swans moving lethargically. Everything in nature was in harmony. The brick wall of the university building across the street seemed powerful but unattainable to her. She asked me to come with her into the building to look for new announcements. We climbed the stairs and found our way through a maze of corridors until we reached the Economics college.

Eva stopped at the bulletin board where she found the announcement indeed. She was not admitted to the University.

She stood next to the board for a few minutes and then turned her pale face to me.

"Would you come with me to the Dean?" She asked.

"Of course." But I knew that this will be a useless quest. The Dean's secretary made us wait for two hours. In the meantime, another woman entered and sat down.

"This is the third time I've come to see the Dean. Don't expect much. He's so unfriendly that he doesn't even let you into his office. He blocks the entrance with his body. You'll get nothing from him."

"I don't expect much, but we have to try," I replied.

We had invested so much time in waiting, we were not about to leave now. All my thoughts were focused on what tactics to take with this man.

Finally, the secretary grudgingly called our names. Just as we were warned, the Dean stood in the frame of the doorway. Eva and I greeted him in Latvian. His stern face relaxed. He answered our greeting with an invitation into his office, a handsome room with high ceilings and wide windows overlooking the tree-lined canal.

He gestured for us to sit down.

"How can I help you?" He asked.

I answered his question with a question as Jews do when they study Talmud.

"Is it fair to someone who was born and raised in Riga to be refused acceptance into the Latvian University?"

"My hands are tied," he answered defensively. "I had an order from the Ministry of Higher Education to accept two students from the Azerbajan Republic." After a moment of silence he said, "I will speak to the Ministry. Have Eva come on Monday at noon."

Eva was shy but I shook his hand vigorously when we said our grateful thank-yours.

On September 1, 1970, Eva called me at work.

"I am accepted!" She yelled into the phone.

It was a Riga miracle. But the young Jewish generation did not want to go on living by miracles.

****

CHAPTER VIII

HOPE

The Influence of Israeli Victory

In Riga Jewish youths cheer. The Latvians support Israel. The Russians condemn the aggressors. The Soviet government dissolves diplomatic relations with Israel. It is a remarkable victory, this six-day war in Israel.

After 1967, during the year that followed, Soviet Jews gained a renewed confidence and strong Jewish identity. By the end of the year, thrilling news is splashed across the newspapers. Headlines read.

Young Riga Jews high-jack a plane in Leningrad—Destination—Israel.

We are all shocked. Bravery of this kind had never before been seen in the Soviet Union. The story unfolds…

A loyal Soviet citizen—a spy had penetrated the group of Jewish dissenters. He immediately reports to the KGB. Great publicity. A trial. Punishment. Severe sentences for most; death sentences for the others. The names of the heroic men and women: Zalmanson, brother and sister; Mendelevich, brother and sister; Knoch, Penson. There were others.

These courageous people, now in their fifties, are living in Israel. But this was a natural revolt that the idea of an escape to Israel found its roots in Riga where the majority of Latvian Jews were fiercely Zionists. Since the founding of Israel in 1948, there were always Baltic Jews who continuously applied for exit visas. Even though they were most often denied, they applied again and again. Once or twice a year a family or two would get permission to leave, but for the most part the Soviet dictatorship did not let their people out, not even to travel abroad. When foreign tourism finally developed, the group leader would be always a KGB officer to watch and restrict communications with foreigners. The Russians blocked new ideas from coming in, in the same way they shielded the truth about themselves from the world.

The shock was indescribable when in March of 1971, fifteen families were called into the visa department of the Riga Internal Affairs Ministry. They were offered permission to leave on short notice, if they wished. This news spread throughout the city like a tidal wave. People were confused because again, anything like this had never happened before. It was hard to catch "The voice of America" or the "BBC Broadcasting" to find out the truth behind these unusual developments.

Even though many Rigans had invitations from relatives to come to Israel, they were afraid to apply, not trusting the Russian oligarchy which they feared would exert power against the Jews. But now the

Riga Jews rushed to prepare all the required papers. The postal service was jammed with letters and telegrams to Israel requesting visas.

As we all did, the reader must wonder, why, on one hand, the Russians opened the doors for Jews to leave, while, on the other hand, they created obstacles. The answer was simple in its complexity.

The promise of the "Most Favored Nations Status" was too powerful to refuse.

A great number of Jews from all over the Soviet Union joined the Baltic Jews in their quest to emigrate. The results of the mass emigration requests caused chaos for the Soviets. They did not realize how many Jews would apply. Soviet science, medicine, technology would miss the Jewish brain. To stop emigration the Soviet government levied an unattainably high tax under the guise of education.

Nothing could stop the Jews. They managed with Jewish American money to pay off the government. However, soon this tax was revoked when it became known that it was largely through economic pressure from the United States.

Right then and there our daughters decided what the future of our family would be. There was no doubt that we would emigrate, we could not miss this once-in-a-life-time opportunity. Humanity had finally raised its voice for us. Jewish community of the free world were reaching out to us.

There were serious complications for the Gurevich family as a consequence of my transfer to another factory. It happened this way: a new factory was built on the basis of a few VEF shops which manufactured telephone equipment for the army. I was soon invited by Lev Davidovich who left VEF to become President of the new factory. He offered me a managerial position to be in charge of the production planning bureau. I accepted the offer because the salary was better. This advancement would cost me now. First, I had to quit my job, and even though Pinya did not have the same high-risk security job that I had, he would also have to quit his job for a "deserter of the country" could not be permitted to supervise workers. We could not risk being left without income, so we had to find jobs first then apply for visas. Besides, Eva was in her first year in the university, she too would have been dismissed as others were for applying to leave the Soviet Union. It became known that many Jews were refused emigration visas. The "refusnicks," as they were called, suffered for many years before finally they were given exit visas. We tried to avoid being in this situation at great cost.

As fate is the final decision-maker, I became ill with a sudden itching that would not go away. There was no diagnosis established and no cure. After two years of suffering, thanks to my old VEF connections, I got into the best hospital in Moscow. I had a liver disorder, but they too had no medicine for it, although they knew that Questran could help me. I continued to scratch myself until I drew blood, but the itching would not stop. I was in such physical anguish that I asked my cousins Ben and Tanya to send me the Questran from the United States. Here I confronted another obstacle: the Soviet Union restricted drugs of any kind being shipped in from abroad. I lived in a nightmare that would not end. It became impossible for me to remain in Riga, nevertheless, I was afraid to take a wrong step. Our children's lives were at stake. We could not ask anyone for advice because we didn't know what rules the Soviets were playing.

In addition to our unstable situation, we had no money to cover the expenses emigration required. Pinya started looking for additional sources of income. He saw that there were teams of workers who would provide the packing for the emigrants, but Pinya was shy to offer his help at first. Slowly he too started getting clientele and had to do this job after his regular work at the factory, a less responsible position at "VEF." Pinya soon became busy; he worked to exhaustion but it did not provide enough money to emigrate.

Our oldest daughter, Anna worked as an English teacher in a high-school in the town of Sigulda. She would come home only for weekends. One winter night she told us that she met a man by the name of Edward Gershenson, an electronic engineer also at the VEF factory.

Edward grew up in the Urals never being aware that he was Jewish until once he heard the boys in the street making fun of Jews. Ed came home disturbed and asked his parents, "Am I a Jew?"

"Yes."

"Why didn't you tell me?"

"Who told you about that?" They asked.

"The boys."

Ed's mother, Clara, was head physician of the local hospital where her Jewishness was not an issue. She was a good doctor, that's all anyone cared about. Anti-Semitism had not reached their town yet. However, Ed could not accept this kind of insults, and even though he was a top student, he wanted to leave his hometown. So, he moved to Sverdlovsk, but could not find peace there either. This surge of Jewish identity brought him to Riga where pre-Soviet customs, traditions and life style were still preserved. The time came when Ed became interested in Riga Jewish novelties and decided to emigrate.

On the day of Anna's 25-th birthday, Ed came to our home with a bouquet of roses in his hands and a proposal. Anna agreed to become his wife. He knew nothing of Jewish tradition. Pinya and I arranged a wedding, which would take place under a huppa. Again caution had to be applied. We invited our relatives and the most trusted friends and guests who were leaving for Israel in a few days. My aunt Mira and Semyon refused to come for the huppa. They were among the guests who were invited for the reception. Our gorgeous bride with the handsome groom followed their friends who held lit candles in silver candelabras. The flower girl strew field flowers over the path of the newlyweds. A five-piece orchestra played the joyous Jewish wedding music. Guests who were standing on both sides passed their roses to the bride. The receiving ceremony ended with a freilechs inviting for the Chasidic dance. The Russian "P" type long tables were set for the delicious food. The feast had begun.

****

We knew we could not apply yet. We also needed money. Only to give up Soviet citizenship required a large sum besides the cost of foreign passports, tickets, fixing your apartment and numerous other expenses. I had no choice other than ask Ben for financial help. It was a hard task for me. Of course, Ben helped me.

****

It is 1974. We celebrated Shulamit's first birthday. Next day Ed initiated a conversation that would begin a new push. We were not ready yet. We feared that we be refused; we feared to spoil Eva's future. Ed and Anna were determined, they were going to leave without us. I was in panic: I may never see my child again. Everyday, we heard rumors floating through the air that the Russians were closing the borders. The children rushed to apply. It was on a slippery winter morning on my way to work, deeply in thoughts about our separation. I sled and fell on the ice. I was taken to the hospital where I remained in bed for six weeks.

The day arrived, the bitter sweet day arrived. I could hardly walk. I still could not sit. My friends helped me prepare my last dinner for my children. I wanted them to leave from our home, from my cooking, from my dinner table, from my thoughts. Our last dinner was of stuffed cabbage. I could not hold back my tears. Our little granddaughter was twenty one months old. I prayed that God grants me the privilege to watch her grow. Dinner was over. It was time to leave, time to go to the train terminal. I stood next to the train trying not to cry, not to give into the weakness of a mother's love. The train will take off in five minutes. I took my daughter's hand.

"I will fly on my wings to you, my child."

I knew it would not be an easy flight.

Recipe

Stuffed Cabbage:

Prepare filling:

Grind two pounds of beef with an onion

Cook 1 glass of rice in 2 cups boiled water

Add 1 tbs. chopped parsley

Combine the ingredients adding salt and pepper to taste

Put one Cabbage head in a pot with boiled water for 10 minutes

Take it out, let the water drain

Separate each leaf, cut out thick part of cabbage leaf

Stuff each cabbage leaf with the filling

Fold over and roll

Fry each roll for a few minutes on each side

Place the rolls in a roasting pan, cover with ground carrots

and tomatoes. Pour over 1 glass of water

Bake for one hour at 350 degrees

In a hot sauce pan add 4 tbs. sugar

Move the pan around (do not stir the sugar)

When the sugar is brown add 1 cup water and 1 tbsp. sour salt

Make the sweet and sour sauce to your taste and pour over the cabbage rolls

Bake for another 45 minutes

Serve with hot boiled potatoes.

Our Emigration

As all the graduates, Eva was assigned by the university to her first job where she was to begin within a week. But we anticipated a problem: she needed a letter of recommendation in order to apply for an exit visa.

"Why do you need this letter? "The chief of human resources asked her.

"I am applying for an exit visa." She answered.

"Sit down and listen to me." He leaned across the desk. "I will not give you the letter. I don't want to get into trouble. But I will do something for you. I will not force you to stay and work off the time you owe us for your education."

Eva and I went to the housing department together to ask for two letters. I had not returned to work after my back injury. So, Eva and I were both unemployed now.

In most cases the providers of the letters, volunteers devoted to the Soviet system, were addicted to the anguish of the oppressed emigrants. In order to apply for a visa you had to have a letter of recommendation along with a mountain of papers that we had somehow to obtain. The letters were only one part of all the other humiliations we had to endure before the papers were given to us. The sole purpose of the letters was to shame us. The Housing volunteers orally bashed us, calling us traitors.

"This country fed you and this is the thanks we get for our gracious hospitality."

They fed us lies about emigrants who returned home disappointed. We accepted their abuse with stoicism because we knew that they had to give us the letters anyway. On the other hand, Pinya received the letter from his workplace easily. His bosses were loyal to him.

Finally, the lucky moment arrived when the three of us went to apply for our visas. As hard as it was to wait four years for the day we could apply, it was much harder to count each day and each night of the next four months before we received the post-card with our appointment.

Our day started by running back and forth downstairs to check on our mailbox. The two precious letters we were waiting for were from Anna and from the visa department. Anna's letters would come seldom because the Soviet system had a habit to keep foreign letters in the main post office without delivering them to their addressee.

I had learned a trick then; other Jews would go to the post office and complain about the delay of their letters. The clerk then pretended to be nice and as a big favor check on the letters, then he would come out and bring a few letters without ant apology. However, nobody knew of any tricks to use for the visa department.

On that lucky Monday morning, Eva ran downstairs to check the mail box and returned swiftly with a post-card in her hand. This was the long awaited invitation from the visa department.

The trolley was close by. Within twenty minutes we were climbing the stairs toward a beautiful future, stairs that were to us in the most powerful building in Riga, the building that held the visa department. My thoughts ran ahead of me. Every step brought us closer to our children, to Anna, Edward and Shulamit. I craved to see my children. The memories of all the bad Soviet years slipped away.

Each step up, the words rang in my imagination "Da, Nyet, Da, Nyet."

Da, you may receive your visa to leave. Nyet, you are refused.

"Nyet," said the woman behind a heavy oak desk.

My crystal hopes were shattered by despair and disbelief. Still I had enough presence of mind to ask the clerk for the reason. She gave no explanation.

"Let's go to Aunt Mira." I said to Eva.

I wanted to cry my heart out and Mira lived near-by. So many times in the past she would help me reach a solution to a problem. This time she had no advice for me. They were devoted to the "party." They did not approve of our decision even though, she said,

"I understand your pain."

Eva and I sat there for a long time. I cried. I screamed. They will close the borders any day. I will never see my child again. Eva listened to me and then she said:

"Mamochka, you must calm down. I know you will come up with a solution."

Her words were like magic. I regained my strength, ready again for the struggle.

I wrote letters to government officials. I booked appointments. But these channels did not work. Finally, I decided to take a different, a more dangerous approach. I went to see Grisha Tetz, the attorney of the factory, which I had left four and a half years earlier. He opened the door of his apartment and welcomed Pinya and me warmly. We chatted for a while. We became re-acquainted. I asked him of what to do about my security clearance. He then told me the name of the man in whose hands our destiny would lie. His name was Ivan. He was officially an engineer in the factory but in reality he was a KGB colonel in charge of state security. I barely knew him. I would see him passing along the long narrow hallway. He never looked me in the eye. We never spoke.

I no longer slept for more than two or three hours a night, and my troubled sleep slashed through with nightmares. Only my English studies helped to relax my mind.

Everything fell into place. I started to focus my thoughts on how I could approach the KGB man.

On one of my sleepless nights, Ekaterina appeared in my thoughts. I saw her two years earlier in the Gas Company where I found an accounting job after I left the factory. I didn't feel comfortable then speaking to her because I feared she would ask me for the reason I had left my good job in the factory. I thought she didn't see me, so I pretended not to see her. However, a few days later, Ekaterina walked into my office and came right to the point of her visit.

"Could you help me to get a gas stove."

Her request did not surprise me because it was the Russian way. In most societies, it's not what but who you know. The old adage applied here, as well.

"I am not involved with the supply department." I answered.

"It is hard for me without gas in the kitchen. I have the pipes, I just need a stove." She implored.

"I will try to speak to the supply manager even though I don't know her. Wait here."

I left my office and went to the supply department. Luckily the manager was there. She was a middle aged Latvian woman who I spoke

Latvian to. She looked at her schedules and gave me an immediate answer.

"Yes, she would find a stove."

I was thrilled that I could help Ekaterina, who thanked me profusely. I could feel the glance of her clever eyes at me, then she left without asking any questions.

I had not seen her since that incident and didn't know where she lived. I knew that she was in charge of the secret documents in the factory. Even though we had a strictly working relationship, I thought she might help me to approach Ivan, the KGB man. I did not disclose my plans to either Pinya or to Eva, but decided to find Ekaterina on my own.

It was a rainy morning when I left the house for the Address Information Bureau of the city of Riga. Near the train terminal was a single kiosk where I had to speak through a tiny slot window. From behind the window a woman handed me an application. All I could write down was Ekaterina's name. I left the other questions blank. When the clerk took my application, she shrugged her shoulders and said:

"Come back in an hour, but I doubt if I'll be able to find the address with so little information."

I walked the autumn streets in the rain. Then I returned to the kiosk. The clerk reached out from inside. Her hand held my application. I exclaimed when I saw the box filled in with Ekaterina's address.

I knew Riga very well. However, I was not that familiar with this distant poor neighborhood. I caught the tram that would take me once again on the first step toward freedom.

Leaving the tram, I walked in the downpour along slippery cobbled streets until I finally found Ekaterina's address. Her small apartment house stood in a shabby courtyard. I stepped in and found her first floor apartment. I rang the bell, but no one answered. I decided to try another flat. A woman opened the door. Excessively talkative and open, she gave me the information I needed. "Ekaterina will be home at six o'clock tonight. She's not with the factory anymore," news that cast a shadow on my hopes. I returned home with more determination to settle our problems, even more monumental seemed the solutions. So, before twilight, I left my home again and stopped at the best pastry shop in town. From there I took the tram to Ekaterina's. I rang her door bell. There was no answer. However, the neighbor told me before to check another flat where Ekaterina's friend lived. There I found her.

Ekaterina was surprised, yet still happy to see me. We went to her apartment.

Ekaterina was a middle aged blond Russian, who moved to Riga after the war. She lived with her daughter and granddaughter in rather poor living quarters. With a smile on her lips, she showed me the precious stove that I had helped her obtain. Without asking, in typical Russian hospitality, she brewed a pot of Ceylonskiy chai, the best brand of tea. She took my coat and told me to make myself at home. I handed her the pastry box which she took with delight, like a child, and placed it on the table. I was in fear because she had the power to turn me into the authorities, when I shall ask for her help to emigrate. I didn't know her well enough to think she would not betray me. However, under the circumstance I had to trust someone.

Ekaterina's soft chattering and the hot aromatic tea helped me relax. I still didn't know how to approach her. I knew I had to start somewhere. There was an uncomfortable silence, then finally I spoke into it.

"Did you know that my oldest daughter, with her husband and baby emigrated?"

"No," she replied, "I didn't."

"I too would like to emigrate," I went on. "This was the reason I quit my job from the factory and applied only four years later. I want to see my child and her child."

"I can understand. I too would follow my child." She responded. We were no longer business associates, we were simply two mothers, who loved their children. However, the hardest part lay ahead. I had to make Ekaterina trust me enough to confide in me.

"I was refused an exit visa." I continued, "I came to you, Ekaterina, to find out who would be in charge of releasing my security restrictions?"

"Why don't you go to the president of the factory?" She suggested.

"I believe the KGB should lift the restrictions." I said.

"So, then talk to the chief of the Security Department in the factory."

"I don't think he's in charge." I said. I knew this from the attorney. Another long silence.

Ekaterina went on mentioning names of employees in the Security Department. I kept silent. Then she mentioned Ivan.

"It could be him." I shrugged innocently.

"Listen. Ivan is a good man and he lives near-by. Go and see him right away." She insisted.

This sudden idea frightened me.

"Would you come with me?" I asked.

"No, it would not be appropriate, and..." she went on, "you don't need me as a witness. I will take you there to show the apartment building and the location of his windows."

"What should I say?" I asked Ekaterina. It was not that I didn't know what to say: I just did not know the KGB mind and needed her input.

"Tell him exactly what you told me." She answered.

It was still drizzling outside when Ekaterina changed her slippers for shoes and put on her raincoat. This area was new to me. Poorly constructed houses were built all over the place only to accommodate the large numbers of Soviet secret agents. These men of every rank were sent by the government to hold responsible positions and at the same time to control the Latvian population. The windows, so closely structured to each other, indicated to me that the apartments were small and had low ceilings. There were four apartments on each floor of the five story buildings. The walls were thin, so there was little privacy. Who knows, may be they were built like that for reasons of information control. The high-ranking officials were given comfortable apartments in good neighborhoods.

Ekaterina pointed out the windows of Ivan's apartment and left. Up to that point, she was my guardian angel. Now, I was on my own. It was time to take action. I stood outside this imposing building afraid that someone could see me. Then I stepped inside a dark hallway with the stairs right in front of me. I climbed up a few floors and found the apartment. I touched the bell lightly as if it would bite my hand, but was afraid to ring it. Why was life so easy for some, so complicated for me? I was alone in an unknown place. I took a determined breath and pushed the bell; a friendly middle-aged woman opened the door immediately.

"Does Comrade Ivan live here?" I asked with trepidation.

"Yes. Come in. Come in." Her voice welcomed me.

Ivan appeared in the doorframe of the living room. I recognized him immediately. He looked at me as if he had never seen me before. I re-introduced myself. He was polite.

"Take off your coat and come in," he invited. His wife stood by in obedient silence.

Everyone sat down. More silence. They waited for me to start speaking.

"I don't know how to begin." I told them.

"Just say whatever is on your mind." He answered. "Valyay."

I began my story as if he did not know anything about me. I told them what I had told Ekaterina an hour earlier. I also told them about my itching and the medicine I needed to cure it. He permitted me to talk without interruption. When I finished my story, I asked if he could help me. He didn't say "Da" he did not say "Nyet."

I left their house with hope, although I was not sure in which way he could direct that help.

I arrived home high on my own courage.

"Sit down," I said to Pinya and Eva, "I have something to tell you," and started the fairy-tale. It sounded as unbelievable to me as it was to them. Eva sat in silence. Pinya said, "it's not so simple, this dream of yours."

I wanted to call Ivan every day, but I had to wait for an excuse.

Two months later, on February 23rd, I called Ivan to wish him a happy holiday. It was the anniversary of the Soviet Army.

"I could do nothing," he whispered into the phone, "call again."

He was going to help me. I knew this now.

Two weeks later I called him again. He told me to make an appointment with the personnel department to see the president of the factory. I knew that he wanted the president to invoke the request of security clearance. I was afraid to put him in danger. He was a Jew. He was the only person in whom I entrusted with the reason I had to quit my job four and a half year ago. He tried to persuade me then to stay and not seek emigration. I told him that this was our children's decision. Soon after, I left my job. Now I had to ask him for a favor. I knew he would not be open to the request, but I had no alternative.

My concern disappeared the minute I walked into the reception room. The same two secretaries, Raisa and Tonya welcomed me with the same warmth as they always had in the past.

"Lev Davidovich will see you now, Roda Savelyevna." Raisa said.

The chief of personnel department sat next to my friend, the attorney. The president invited me to sit down opposite them.

"It has been a long time since I left the factory." were the words with which I began the conversation. They listened as I spoke.

"You might argue that I had an important job, but it has been almost five years. I don't know what's going on in the factory now. I'm sure everything's changed… I only want to be with my children and grandchild."

The president sat back in his chair and sighed; I watched the attorney as he squirmed in his seat; the chief of personnel had been taking notes through the entire conversation.

Finally, the president stood up from his chair and said to the chief personnel: "Review her records."

We all stood up. I knew he was afraid to even shake my hand out of fear of showing friendship in front of the other KGB personnel in the room.

Three weeks later there was a card in our mailbox. It was from the visa department for an appointment. Permission was granted for us to leave. Eva could not stop crying. This time it was I who had to calm her down. Pinya received the good news with a shade of uncertainty. How would we start life anew? That same evening I took Pinya with me to see Ivan.

"We came to thank you," I said.

"You don't have to thank me," he replied.

We handed him a bottle of the best "Crystal" vodka. He refused it.

"When you are reunited with you daughter and have your first drink with her, raise your glasses to the simple Russian Ivan."

Worcester

On a warm August morning in 1976, we landed at the tiny airport in Worcester, Massachusetts. Anna, Ed and Shulamit were there. Selma Levy and Ilsa Rothchild from the Jewish Federation accompanied them. The same evening I raised my glass to Ivan.

"Za zdravye." Our family replied in joyous unison.

Many times we have lifted our glasses to Ivan, our simple Russian Savior.

CHAPTER IX
EIGHTEEN YEARS LATER

Apple Pie

Recipe

Pie Pastry:

2 cups flour

.5 tsp. salt

.5 cup butter

2 tsp. sugar

1 egg

4 tbs. cold water

Sift flour with salt into a bowl

Cut butter into flour in small pieces

Rub in with the fingertips until mixture looks like crumbs.

Make a well in the center and add sugar, egg and water.

Stir to combine.

Draw flour into mixture in the center quickly with a knife.

Press together with fingers, adding more water if necessary.

Turn onto a floured board and knead lightly for a few seconds.

Wrap in wax paper, chill for 30 minutes.

Filling:

6 tart apples

.5 cup sugar

1 tbs. cornstarch

.5 tsp. cinnamon

.25 tsp. nutmeg

1 tbs. lemon juice

1 tbs. butter

Peel, core and slice apples into bowl and stir with sugar, cornstarch, cinnamon and nutmeg until apple slices are well coated

Divide pastry and roll half into a circle to line pie pan

Fill pie with apple mixture, leveling the top

Sprinkle with lemon juice and dot with butter

Roll out the remaining pastry to cover the pie

Seal and decorate edges, brush the top with water

Bake in a hot oven 425 degrees for 10 minutes

Reduce heat to 350 degrees and continue baking for 40 minutes

Or until crust is brown

On an unusually cool New England day in July 1994, Pinya burst into my American kitchen, waving papers in the air.

"Rodinkah, we're going to Riga."

The kitchen was alive with color and smells from fresh flowers, apples and cinnamon. I looked up from the bowl filled with dough: I was making an American apple pie. I wiped my flour-covered hands on my apron and said in answer to his obvious joy.

"Are you crazy? Why now? Our eighteen year celebration in the United States is coming up."

"I want to go back for a visit. We have unfinished business there." He wanted to visit his parents and brother's grave; I have things to do also. I would finally be able to thank Ivan for helping us escape from the "Motherland."

"We'll celebrate our Chai party when we get back."

"OK," I nodded to my dear Pinya and raised my hands in concession. "I'll think about it." I still held on to my old fear. But Pinya was determined, so became I, and besides, he had already booked the trip.

****

Since there was no direct flight from either Boston or New York, we would fly by way of Copenhagen. I could finally satisfy my long-time wish to meet the Danish people who had saved Jews from the Nazis.

The tough reality of our lives eighteen years ago was still fresh in my memory, even though I hoped it was different now when Latvia had recently gained independence. When I go back, I thought, I'll go back as an American. I would travel in jeans, a costume I had never worn before. They were a symbol that to me represented freedom, and to my surprise, I looked pretty good in them. What was important, it felt natural; I felt great.

After changing planes in London, we boarded the plane for Copenhagen. I sat next to the window. Pinya sat in the middle next to an older Danish man who immediately engaged him in a conversation. The flight took only ninety minutes, so the conversation was brief. But to our surprise we saw the man again, standing with a cart filled with luggage, and with another empty cart. He was waiting to help us. This was the reputed Danish hospitality about which we had heard.

Copenhagen spread out over two islands; Zealand and Amagen, which are in the thirteen-mile wide Sounds at the entrance to the Baltic Sea. I looked for similarities between Riga and Copenhagen. The only similarities I found were the narrow streets, and the language that had related inflections. I wanted to learn more about the people, but we were hungry. We were also eager to taste the Danish herring, similar to the Latvian. We found it on the famous Stroget Street.

After dinner we continued our walk to the Danish Royal Theater to see "Tornrose" (The Sleeping Beauty), by Tchaikovsky. We were lucky to get the last two available seats, albeit separate, on the third balcony. I gave the better seat to Pinya because I wanted to honor him. Soon the first familiar chords of the overture brushed past my ears, sweeping me away when the curtains opened to the beautiful Russian palace in which the heroes and heroines of Charles Parrault's tale began their gorgeous dance celebrating Aurora's birth. During intermission, I went to visit Pinya where once again he was in conversation with a young Dane. The man stood up when Pinya introduced me to him and so gallantly offered his seat. I thanked him saying that I would return to my place before the intermission was over. He tried to convince me to stay, explaining that even my bad seat will be better for him because he could see the orchestra from there. I accepted his generous offer.

The lights dimmed, Pinya took my hand and together we were on a woody glen with the royal hunting party. Together we celebrated romance. When Aurora and the Prince married, Pinya and I were again one.

The ballet over, we went out into the fresh air of the festive Copenhagen night. It was late and we had another day to enjoy in this fairy-tale city. Our taxi driver asked us how we liked "Tornerose." Everyone seemed excited about "Tornerose" and pleased that we went to see it. It appeared that the entire city of Copenhagen celebrated the ballet.

Our comfortable bed in the hotel welcomed us after a sleepless night of travel.

We were ready for the new day. The first thing on our agenda was the synagogue but much to my distress, we overslept. We dressed hurriedly, took a bite of breakfast, and rushed out of the hotel. Even though we had a city map and knew that the Synagogue was within walking distance, we had to ask for directions. A young man on the street patiently explained to us how to get there. But again to our surprise he pulled out his business card and offered his help in the city if we should need it. Overwhelmed by his generosity, I asked Pinya to take a picture of him.

Shacharit was over, the synagogue was closed, we could only observe the gray old building from behind the iron fence.

We spent the rest of the day in the glamour of the Tivoli Gardens.

****

It was time for Riga. The small hall that boarded for Riga was grim in comparison to the generous and elegant charm elsewhere. This was a precursor.

People were reading Latvian newspapers all around us but Pinya and I continued to speak English. I did not feel the excitement I thought I would in returning to my home. Instead I felt old apprehension. I knew nothing would be the same. Everything and everyone I held dear were in the United States: my family, my friends, my work.

The flight was short. After the complimentary drinks, the conversations grew loud. Latvian and German were the only languages spoken. In two hours, we landed in our homeland, Riga. As we walked down the ramp, an older heavy man asked me.

"Are you from London?"

"No, I'm not."

"Are you Latvian?"

"No, I am Jewish," I said with conviction knowing that if I were a Latvian citizen instead of an American citizen, the word "Jew" would be on my passport. Before we arranged for our visas, another crowd of passengers lined up next to us. I recognized them to be Russians by their somber faces. A young Latvian customs officer with an angry face finally permitted us into the airport hall where our daughter Eva's university friend, Tanya, waited for us. Next to her was Bella, my childhood friend, with her son Ilja. Our joyous reunion erased my tension. We were to stay in Tanya's and her husband Mark's apartment.

The Mercedes in which Tanya had arranged to pick us up, pulled out from the airport into the main road to the city: "Kalnciema Street," a street of a few kilometers. But our ride past the gloomy ill kept buildings seemed unending. The absence of cars and people gave the street a death-like demeanor. Finally we approached the Daugava River and the bridges connecting two parts of Riga. We continued down Valdemara Street, which brought a flood of precious memories to me. They had renamed all the streets with the original pre-Soviet occupation names, a symbol of their new freedom.

The first thing I saw was the great Latvian Academy Theater, the jewel of Latvian culture. It, too, stood silent and empty. Next, we passed the red brick building of the Latvian Academy of Art. Since it was late summer, it was also emptied of students. A block further, at the corner of "Elizabetes" stood the Art Museum, which eighteen years ago seemed to us a mighty building where the Soviet government forced us to have our precious china appraised and taxed before leaving the country.

I remember how they impounded my mother's Kuznetsov china, so dear to me for I found it after returning to Riga at the end of World War II.

I wanted to continue down Valdemara Street because we were near the building where my Aunt Mira and Uncle Semyon used to live. But the traffic called for a different route. I asked myself what difference would it make, when I knew that in a few days we will visit their graves at the Rainis Cemetery. In this short journey from the airport, my heart was filled once more with sadness as I witnessed the lost glory of my once dear Riga.

We turned onto Elizabetes Street, the Esplanade was before me. I remembered those years when I walked the alleys with my sweet Anechka in her carriage, side-by-side with my friend Tanya and her little Edochka. The alleys were empty now. Two blocks farther was Vermanya Park, where next to the music pavilion my vigorous Evinka would jump rope with many other children. There was no life there either, except for a lonely pedestrian who walked out of the park, probably cutting through from Merkelya Street. Where had the new Rigan mothers and babies disappeared to? Their absence, this silence was surreal. We drove through Elizabetes Street until we took a left on Krishyana Barona, it still had rails for the trams that ran to the various parts of Riga. This was the first life I saw on the street not wide enough for cars to pass through. Here I noticed a Chrysler dealership, which I later learned belonged to Ilja and his friend Sergey. We were close to Tanya's place on Bruninieku, but could not get there directly because it was a one way street. This gave us the opportunity to see more of Riga. What we saw was a city that was shabby and worn down, no trace of the once free and elegant Riga of my childhood memories. Finally, we approached Tanya's apartment house. Vladik, their handsome fourteen-year old son, gave us an enthusiastic welcome. Mark, his father, held a managerial position at a club, he was in charge of a gala concert-competition between the Italian guests and local singers.

I felt dispirited on my first day in Riga. This was the capital of Latvia, my birthplace, a city with a population of close to a million, and yet empty of Jews. There were but a handful of people left still precious to me. If not for them and the others waiting for us in their graves, I would have turned around and gone home that same day.

****

It was Lyalya whom I called first.

Lyalya came into our lives when on a cold Baltic summer day in 1952, the bell rang in our apartment. It was a telegram from the Chukotski peninsula, a place near the North Pole, delivered to our neighbors, Nadezhda Samuilovna and Timofey Dmitrovich. Lyalya's father, Sasha, informed his in-laws that their daughter had died and he was flying the four-month old baby to Riga. Pinya and I shared this great tragedy with our neighbors and waited with them for the baby to arrive. When Sasha appeared at the door he was drunk. In his arms, he held a little bundle wrapped in a gray woolen shawl. Sasha spent most of his fortune to buy plane tickets. He spent the rest of the money he earned from working in a horrible job, in a horrible climate, on alcohol. He stayed for a brief visit, then left without the baby. The grandparents adopted the child. "Lyalya" became the precious word, raised and beloved as if she were one of my children. Even though she was baptized, she adopted many traditions of our Jewish way of life; when we were about to emigrate, she took our separation very hard. In all we spent twenty-three years as neighbors and friends who had shared the same apartment, the same hard life.

Lyalya, now a tall thin blond woman in her early forties arrived to see Pinya and me. In her hands, she held a bouquet of freshly cut flowers. Her eyes were already filled with tears when I ran to hug her. I had no words; Lyalya could not speak either. We swayed back and forth in our embrace. Then Pinya came over to greet her. We finally sat down at Tanya's graciously set table, but Lyalya was shy and would not have a bite until Tanya persuaded her to eat.

I could not take my eyes off this young woman whom I had not seen for eighteen years. Her harsh life had caused her face to shrink, and her palms and fingers to expand. I wanted to hold her, to hug her, to lift up her spirit. But it was not possible. She would stay in Riga; I would not.

Next I had to find Ludmila Bastina, my Aunt Mira's only surviving friend who took care of my aunt's and uncle's graves. She was a retired prosecuting attorney who had once lived a life of Soviet luxury, now barely surviving on a small pension which did not even pay her rent. I found Ludmila after a four-day search. Next, I needed to find my old colleague, Anna Platupe, with whom I had stayed in touch, although she had not answered my last letter. I assumed she was out of town visiting her family. I invited Lyalya to join me in the search for Anna.

While we walked, I listened to Lyalya's story.

If not for her husband, Tolya, who luckily found a temporary job, she could hardly make ends meet. Lyalya was cleaning hallways and bathrooms in a hotel every other day. She hoped to be assigned to room cleaning which could give her additional income in tips.

"Why would they give you that job?" I asked her.

"Because nobody speaks English in this hotel. They found out that I knew some English, so whenever they need a translator for the foreign guests, they call me."

"Couldn't you get a better job?" I asked her.

"I'm lucky to have this job. Rodochka, don't you know what's going on here? There are no jobs. The factories are closing one after another. They closed the factory where I was working in the cafeteria as a cashier."

"Why?" I asked. She threw out her hands impatiently.

"There's no raw material to produce goods, so there's nothing to sell. The old ties with Russia don't exist anymore, and we have no foreign currency to buy material from the West.

"This isn't America," she said with an edge to her voice. "No one takes care of us with welfare or unemployment. If we're hungry, there are no food-stamps to fill our stomachs."

I felt a moment of misplaced guilt, and then said quietly, " I worked hard in America and still do." I still felt sorry for her plight.

No-one answered Anna's door bell. We stood in her court-yard hoping that a neighbor would appear from the building who might know where she was. No one came out; no one entered. Finally, we saw an old woman walking slowly toward the building. Her legs were badly swollen. As I approached her, I spoke in Latvian, a language I had hardly used in the past eighteen years. The neighbor must have trusted me, otherwise she would not have invited us into her fifth floor apartment next to my friend Anna's. To my great luck, the woman had Anna's niece phone number.

I wanted to call Anna right away, but I was shy to ask the neighbor. Guessing my thoughts, this kind woman offered to make a call.

Would Anna recognize my voice? I asked myself, as I dialed the number. Anna's niece answered the phone.

"Vai es ludzu varu runat ar Jusu tanti?" I asked in Latvian.

["Hello," I said, may I please speak to your aunt?"]

It felt strange standing in my old shoes. It was as if I were a character in my own suspense novel. Then I heard Anna's uneasy voice.

"Kas runa?" ["Hello, who is this?"]

"Ka Tev klajas?" ["Anninya? Hello! How are you?"]

"Tu esi seit?" she shouted. ["Rodinya! You are here!"]

"Tu pazini manu balsi? mans mils draugs, es sorit atbraucu un gribu Tevi redzet."

["You recognized my voice, my dear friend, I have just arrived this morning and I want to to see you."]

"Es atbrauksu rit norit ar pirmo autobusu. Es busu kopa ar Tevi visu laiku."

["I will catch the first bus and return to Riga. I will be all the time next to you."] She cried into the phone.

I thanked Anna's neighbor and we left. Lyalya and I returned home victorious. She stayed with us late into the night, we promised to visit her before we left.

****

Our First Rigan Night

Tanya, Pinya and I were alone. Mark had not returned from the club yet. Vladik went to bed.

"Come. We'll sit on the sofa," Tanya invited. The coffee table was set with pechenya [cookies] and a pot of hot tea. We were all tired, but happy to be together, so we just sat and dunked our cookies into the tea.

Tanya had been unusually quiet on this night.

"Are you tired?" I asked her. "You seem preoccupied."

She answered with a shrug and handed me a folder of Xeroxed papers.

"What's this?" I asked as I took the documents out of the folder. "Vilyaki" I mumbled to myself, moving closer to Pinya.

Although everyone knew by word of mouth about the horrors of World War II, here in our hands was a copy—with names and dates of the villains and designers of Hitler's Latvian Holocaust. Here we held the names of the murderers of Pinya's family.

I trembled as I read this document that Mark obtained from the Latvian Historical Archives. Here was the inventory list of the goods and property of Pinya's parents, claimed and nationalized by the Soviet government after they invaded Latvia in 1940. The paper was fifty-four years old, yet it read as clearly as if it had just been written.

I scanned it from top to bottom until my eyes reached the signatures. The name on the list was of Pinya's father whom I had never known and whose photograph I had never seen. Here was his clear and beautiful signature as if he were still alive.

The next document was a testimony signed by four people of Pinya's town of Vilyaki who witnessed and described the massacre down to the smallest details; the massacre in which my husband's parents, brother, aunts, uncles, cousins, friends and town's people were murdered.

The Testimony

This is a translation. See appendix for original Russian document.

On January of 1945, a document of testimony was filed at the Latvian Historical Archives. It was written by four people who lived in the town of Vilyaki, Latvia, witnesses of Hitler's Latvian Holocaust. They were Vladimir Tikhonov; Zinaida Mazikina; Georgy Kuznetsov; Janis Lonin.

It is a testimony of the atrocities committed on a people who remained in Vilyaki after the Germans occupation on July 3, 1941.

During the first days of the occupation, massive arrests took place.

The victims were thrown into jail.

The butchers   performed inhuman savagery in exterminating the

Jewish population of Vilyaki.

Vilyaki witnessed the cruel beating of the Jews.

Jews were forbidden to walk on the sidewalks of the village.

They were ordered to sew onto their backs and chests the Star of David.

They were allowed to show up in the village only in groups and only for

two hours, from 4 to 6 p.m.

A German Feldfebel (an army rank) walked up and down the village streets.

If a Jew appeared, he murdered him on spot.
[Testified by Yushko, citizen of Vilyaki.]

The Germans did not even have mercy for the Rabbi. They cut off his beard.

[Testified by citizen Makulovich]

On July 1941, the Germans had driven all the Jews to a "Ghetto"

-imprisonment camp, which was located between Balvu and Liepinieku Streets. Armed fascists guarded the Ghetto. Hunger and dirt reigned there.

No medical assistance had been provided for the Jews who were cooped up in cattle-sheds.

Drunken Germans would burst into the ghetto to mock them.

Glazman Yankel had two daughters, ages sixteen and eighteen.

Germans were frequent visitors there. They would order Yankel

face a corner wall, put an armed soldier next to him and rape

these two beautiful young girls over and over again.

[Testified by Yushko Valerian]

The other Germans lined the Jews up in columns and drove them to the a place where they were forced to do filthy jobs, difficult and demeaning. Germans sent a group of girls to clean the soldiers barracks. They ordered the girls to undress. Then they beat them with cudgels and ordered them to swim in the lake.

After swimming they were beaten again and driven to clean the barracks.

[Testified by Yushko]

On the night of August 11, 1941, all the men from the Ghetto were

driven to the fire-depot while all women were ordered to the synagogue

From there, the victims were driven to the police station on

Narodnaya Street for registration. The Jews were condemned to death.

In the police station, their valuables were appropriated.

The witness, Mazikin, saw jewelry piled up on the table.

On August, 1941, at 4:00 in the morning, the Nazi butchers

drove the first group of men to their execution place. They appointed a few men to dig pits. The rest were forced to their knees in a gutter with their backs toward the grave, with arms behind.

They were ordered to lay their heads on the ground where they remained in this position for five hours.

[Testimony given by Mazikin I. N.]

When the pits were ready, a punitive brigade dressed in civil clothing arrived on a blue bus.

Two more cars with German officers arrived at the same time and the same place to take pictures of the shooting scenes.

The murders began to shoot Jews in groups of eight to ten from two submachine guns.

They figured that one bullet should reach the chest, the other bullet should reach the head.

Mothers were ordered to hold their children in their arms as not to waste extra bullets for the child.

The local fascists of Vilyaki by the names of: Valerian Bratushkin, Sosnovski and Gelski finished the shooting of those Jews who were not yet dead.

A local physician by the name of Ilja Mazikin and a paramedic by the name Nuksha were called to be present at the scene of crime in case the murderers needed medical assistance.

Dr. Mazikin testified that one of the butchers with rolled up sleeves came over to him and said:

"I can see that you don't like it, but it is the law that a physician should be present."

The shooting went on until 11:00 a.m. until there was no room in the pits.

New pits were dug by those Jews who would be shot next.

In the meantime, drinks and cigarettes were provided for the murderers.

When new pits were ready, the shooting began again and continued until 3pm until all Jews were murdered.

In this way at this place of the atrocities on August 11 1941, the butchers shot in all, six hundred and fifty innocent people; one hundred and forty five of them were children.

Among these victims were Lithuanian Jews who were caught by the Germans on their way of escape, but had been thrown into Vilyaki Ghetto.

Out of all the murdered, it was possible to recognize only a handful:

> Gurevich Abram   and 3 family members
>
> Gurevich Vulf   and 3 family members

Gurevich Pinchus and wife

Ariks	and 2 family members
Shpitsnadel	and 2 family members
Chernyak	and 6 family members
Bobrov	and 8 family members
Shneer	and 4 family members
Sandler Yevno	and 4 family members
Shishkin	
Sheinis Zavel	and 4 family members
Kapelushnik	and 4 family members
Rochko	
Apanansky	and 3 family members
Abramovich	and 2 family members
Kohan	and 3 family members
Glazman Yankle	and 2 family members
Rabbi Chernyak	and 2 family members
Principal of the Yiddish school	
Teacher Gurevich with family	
Teacher Hiatt	with family
Dentist Getkovich	

Besides the 650 victims, the fascists killed in different times and

places, thirteen more innocent people, one of whom was a child.

Final Death Tally

It has been established and documented that on the territory of Vilyaki and its surroundings, the Germans, with the assistance of the Latvian-German nationalists, had brutally murdered six hundred and sixty three innocent people,   among them one hundred and forty six children.

Dead Horses

In April, 1944 when the German butchers realized that they could not escape from the responsibility of their atrocities, they tried to hide their bloody tracks by taking the following actions according to a witness Anton Bratushkin of the village of Bronti, near Vilyaki.

He testified:

"A death brigade arrived at the place of execution. They were chained, one to the other. They dug the dead out of their graves arranging the corpses in one big pile which they covered with chopped wood. Then they burnt the corpses by pouring a liquid on them. The area of execution had been shielded by tarpaulins. Guards were put on the roads to restrict traffic between Vilyaki and the town of Abrene. A witness by the name Ivanovski joined the witness Bratushkin in his testimony: Dead horses and animal bones together with human ashes were thrown into the empty graves and then covered with soil."

Two graves of five meters long and two meters wide are located within two kilometers from the town of Vilyaki just fifty meters from the fork leading toward Abrene Lugi.

Another grave of fifty meters long and two meters wide is located within hundred meters south of the two above graves.

Here are the names of those who were solely responsible for the Vilyaki massacre:

Hugenberg —German, Chief of police "SD" hauptfurer "SS"

Ritskis —German, Chief of gendarme

Fabricis- —Chief of gendarme

Audzevich —Latvian-German nationalist, chief of police

Kokorevich	—Latvian-German nationalist
Sabolovski	—Latvian-German nationalist
Kuprin	—Latvian-German nationalist
Sosnovski Victor	—Latvian-German nationalist
Bratushkin Valerian	—Latvian-German nationalist
Golski	- Latvian-German nationalist
Romanovski	- Latvian-German nationalist
Baltners	- Latvian-German nationalist
Mekis	- Latvian-German nationalist
Innort	- Latvian-German nationalist
Martinson	- Latvian-German nationalist

Testimony signed:

V. Tikhonov	J. Login
Z. Mazikina	G. Kuznetsov
Seal	

Pinya continued to read the sad story of his beloved. I could not go on reading. I did not want to stay in Riga for one moment more. I sat fascinated in terror, reading this blood-covered document. I wanted to run, to go home. I knew, though, that I could not leave this poisoned ground because there were still things to do. I had an obligation to fulfill; I had to protect my Pinya.

****

Old Friends

The early morning August rain did not last long. The sun dried the wet streets and we were about to leave to visit my friend Bella when the phone rang. Anninya had already arrived. I asked her to come over immediately so she could spend the whole day with us. Even though I knew that her emotions ran high, I could not anticipate that our reunion would be as dramatic as she made it. From the moment she walked in and saw me, I couldn't calm her down. She sobbed, and screamed; she would not let me go. In her ecstasy she did not notice Pinya. "Where's Pinya? He didn't come?"

"Look, Anninya," I said loudly into her eighty-year old deafness. "Pinya is here."

I spoke in Latvian.

"Where is he?' She asked still crying.

As she turned to Pinya, her hugs and cry became even stronger until Pinya said:

"Nomierinajies!" [calm down]. So surprised, she stopped.

I first met Anninya thirty two years ago when I joined the marketing department of VEF, the largest company in Riga. Although Anna was much older than me, we became close friends. Her quiet demeanor, her gentle looks, the sensible expression in her eyes, her excellent work, were all qualities that made me admire and respect her. Gradually our work and personal relationship grew stronger. She didn't have many relatives, nor did she have children from either of her two marriages. She was as devoted to me as if she were my mother. I knew that my visit to Riga would become a sparkling diamond in her dark and lonely life, so I wanted to be with her as much as time would permit. I also had to honor her feelings by not expressing my disappointment with Riga, her precious Latvia.

Anninya and I walked to Bella's place arm in arm. Pinya walked next to us, as we listened to the story of her daily hardships.

The Latvians hated the Soviet occupation. For a half a century they dreamed to gain independence, to bring back their once good life. Unfortunately, their newly-found independence did not fulfill their expectations. Life became worse. The instability in the country made the deficiencies caused by high unemployment and substantial decreases in salaries and pensions impossible to bare. People suffered from hunger and cold which in turn caused a high crime rate to develop. There was another issue which we found out later: the denial of citizenship to those who were not born in Latvia. Since Anninya was a native, this was one less problem for her.

Bella's inviting smile welcomed us into her small apartment. I could have used her sincere friendship in Worcester, however, her family decided to stay on in Riga. Her husband, Chaim, a man overdue for retirement, still held a position in the food industry so it was no surprise that their table was laid with a festive meal of home-made gefilte fish, chopped herring and various salads for appetizers. That would have been enough, but Bella kept bringing more food. A hot meal of sautéed beef for the main course, and then delicious tayglach for desert. This was the Riga hospitality. After dinner we remained at the table and talked about our old friends who immigrated to Israel and to the United States. This emotional retreat to my young years made me forget the reality of Riga today.

We would see Bella and Chaim again, but now we had to leave before dark because we were afraid of muggers. Besides, I knew that the following day would be a hard one for Pinya.

CHAPTER X

VILYAKI: 1994

The Pain

Mark and Tanya had arranged a car for the four of us to go to Vilyaki. We planned to leave at eight o'clock the next morning. Our trip was delayed for two hours for the car broke down the preceding night when the chauffeur returned from another trip. Instead of resting, he had to repair his car. Finally, the door bell rang and the tired chauffeur appeared. Tanya took him to the kitchen to have strong coffee, and then we left.

Being used to our comfortable American automobile, this old shabby Russian car seemed dangerous to me. The engine ground and rattled; the windows were loose, and on top of that, it smelled bad. But I did not complain, I did not want to upset the chauffeur who was trying hard to please us, so I tried to relax. After a half hour of driving, an old saying entered my mind, told me by the famous Raikin: "Do not try to change what is impossible to change." I switched my attention to the beauty of Latvian fields and forests. However, I yearned for the charm of my New England landscape.

We were heading to Pinya's birthplace where he had been raised, and where he had enjoyed his youth until the Soviets invaded Latvia and nationalized his parents store, this store which provided a comfortable living for the family. Moreover, the Soviets did not hesitate to nationalize his family's living quarters as well. KGB officers settled on the second floor of Pinya's house. This was the way Latvia's new rulers, the Russians, stole the people's dignity. Now, after fifty years, the liberated Latvia was going to return the parents property to their son, Pinya. We were getting closer and closer to Vilyaki, a place where the soil had been soaked with blood.

Pinya was sixteen when World War II broke out. In their worst dreams, his parents could not anticipate the tragedy which lay ahead; they hoped that the Germans would return their possessions. Moshe and Chava Gurevich relied heavily on their good Latvian friends with whom they had dealt for their entire lives. Still, Moshe decided that their two teenage sons should leave for a short time until life will become normal again. Pinya's only brother Ruven insisted on staying home. On July 2nd, 1941, Pinya left on his bicycle.

****

It took us more than three hours to get to Vilyaki, a small quiet town. Without Tanya and Mark I would have felt even more frightened. Tanya took a week off from work so that she could devote all of her time to us; so did Mark, he was our guide and protector.

The first thing on our agenda was the Town Hall. We drove into a small yard where a tiny wooden house sat on a well coifed lawn. We received a warm welcome from the young chairman, Marjans Locans, his assistant, Stanislav Puzhulis, from the administrator, Anna, and the land-surveyor, Alexander Ivanov. Two young women were waiting for us outside. Their Chief, Inara Dundure did not show up who would represent a retail chain of the "Latvian Consumer Association," the organization which took over the inventory and goods of Pinya's parents store in 1940 when the Soviets nationalized it. The same organization worked there through the Nazi regime, through the Soviet regime, and now was still working in the same place after Latvia gained independence. Marjans set the agenda for our visit: first he sent us to look at Pinya's property.

I watched as Pinya's face would become pale, his body held demeanor of a beaten man, just yesterday filled with vitality and hope. Here in this place of remembrance, he became confused.

Once it was a beautiful house, now worn-down with age and disparity. The two large apartments, one on each floor, were turned into six tiny apartments. The roof leaked, the floors were unstable. I asked Pinya to get out of there, but it was hard for him to leave his past. I became frightened when a man, drunk with vodka, kept insisting that he had something to tell Pinya.

"Something important," he said slurring his words.

120

"Es nebiju starp tiem fasistiem…" He murmured in Latvian. (I was not among those fascists…)

I pulled Pinya away and together we left this frightening place. We returned to the Town Hall where Marjans asked Anna to set the table. Food and drinks appeared from out of nowhere. And then the country-style tort was presented as if Marjans knew what would please us. Before the meal, Marjans announced the Town Hall's decision to return the house to Pinya.

It was time to go to the mass grave. On this occasion Marjans and Stanislav accompanied the four of us. They had prepared red gladioluses to lay on the grave. Pinya carried his prayer book and yarmolka with him.

We held on to each other, step by step, until we approached the Holy Place. We began to say "Kaddish." I was his tree; he was a leaf on a windy day. I held him up, afraid that he would fall. We bowed in great sorrow, Pinya and I were in agony. It became unbearable to cope with the great catastrophe after we read the testimony and the names of Pinya's dear family that were the victims of the crime. As I write these lines, my heart is filled with pain and disbelief that a race existed who could design this massive ravaging.

The Town's fathers preserve this cite with great care as the monument tells the story in Yiddish, Latvian and Russian. We stood for a while, still holding the flowers, then as we turned to leave this place, Pinya put the flowers down gently in the middle of the vast meadow where his beloved family had been murdered. We took with us the pain that will forever remain part of us.

As we drove back to Riga, I looked dazedly out of the window. Except for the cemetery dwellers, the town was empty of Jews. The land on either side was rich with crop of the new harvest on the lush fields, witness to life that never ends.

****

Daily Life In Riga

The next morning was sunny and warm. Together with Tanya we rushed to the huge Riga farmers' market.

I wished I could have spent the entire day just taking samples of the farmer cheeses and sour creams, but we had to get back. There were so many things left to do in so short a time. We spent our money generously. The local population could not afford to shop as we did. We bought everything in great quantities for our precious guests in Riga. The home-baked rye bread, the yellow cheese with caraway seeds, farmer cheese and sour cream, freshly laid eggs, smoked flounders, wild mushrooms, native tomatoes, sour cherries, red currant, gooseberries and cream candy. We filled our bags to bursting, arms loaded with edible treasure, and dashed to catch a tram home.

We were expecting Celia, my only cousin in Riga, with her daughter Leja to visit us that evening. Since I had not received letters from her for a few years, I thought that she had emigrated to Israel where her step-sister, nieces and nephews lived. All these years, after most of the Jews had left, she remained in Riga. But that night the story she told was about her lack of strength and willingness to make changes. She said she just dragged on with her life as best she could. Even the hopeless know that when there is opportunity one must find strength, so when Celia's grandson returned home from the Soviet Army, he understood that there was no future for Jews either in the anti-Semitic Latvia or in Russia.

Celia was the last Volpyansky to leave Latvia and is now living happily with her family in the state of Israel.

****

Next morning Pinya and I were ready for our business meeting with Inara Dundure, a blond, head-strong woman in her late thirties. She was dressed in a red wool suit. Her long red nails and lips the same shade contrasted with her fair complexion, to give her an overall sense of power. Inara was the branch manager of the Balvi County Consumer Association which held the trust of Pinya's parents' store in Vilyaki. Since she had not been at the meeting in Vilyaki, she came to Riga to meet us. After an hour of discussion, Inara told Pinya that she would return the store to him, and the trust will buy it back. Our negotiations lasted for another two hours at which time, she told us that she will send her attorney to Riga to meet with us with the papers.

****

We completed our "successful" business meeting with Inara. Pinya and I took the number one trolley to Gertrudes Street, it used to be Karl Marx Street under the Soviet regime, no accident was it that they named the next street for Frederick Engels, who was Marx's collaborator in the Communist Manifesto. Even though this ideology never played well in Latvia, its consequences caused irreversible damage to the Latvian population.

We walked through the courtyard of memories, through the door and up the old staircase. There were the same old mailboxes attached to the wall. I stopped to look at our mailbox where eighteen years ago, Eva found the post-card inviting us to pick-up our visas. We climbed the steps and stopped at the door of apartment # 46 and into the two bright rooms in which we raised our dear daughters. To our great pleasure, Timofey Dmitrovich, waited for us along with Lyalya. He remarried after Nadezhda had died, but as he told us, "I visit her grave frequently." We spent a few hours at the cocktail table munching on tiny open sandwiches with coffee and listening to Timofey's stories of the past: the bitter-sweet stories, which we lived through together, and if not for another commitment, I longed to stay here and reminisce my old harsh days with these people.

****

Ludmila Bastina had finally arranged to meet us at the cemetery where my Aunt Mira and Uncle Semyon rested. We did not come with flowers, instead we came with prayer books. Pinya and I stood over their graves and said Kaddish. The reader may remember that they both shared the Communist ideology and therefore wanted to be buried at an International Cemetery, I was not at ease that they did not rest at the Jewish Cemetery, the place where they belonged.

Together with Ludmila and her daughter, Natasha, we placed small pebbles on the graves of my aunt's friends once a distinguished group of people. We proceeded our trip to the Jewish Cemetery in Shmerli where we came to pay respect to our Riga relatives and friends' graves.

****

The Peitavas Synagogue was the only one left standing in Riga after the war. On Shabbat morning we walked the empty, narrow streets in the old part of Riga. A lone pedestrian appeared here and there. We finally reached the cobbled Peitavas Street. The synagogue smelled of fresh paint. Quietly, we opened the door where about fifty old men were sitting in the front rows near the Holy Ark covered with a heavily embroidered velvet curtain. It was painful to witness the lonely synagogue. I looked up to the balcony where voices from the past had echoed, once filled with old and young women. I remembered their faces, their heads covered with silk scarves, with beautiful hats then custom designed for the Yom Tov season, the season when we ask The Almighty to write us into the Book of Life.

****

Ivan, My KGB Angel

Shabbat was over; our festive meal was over; our next hurdle was still ahead.

I had to find Ivan, my KGB man, who had helped us get out of the Soviet Riga eighteen years ago. I did not remember his address or his telephone number and could scarcely recall the location of the building complex where he lived. I only remembered that it was next to the tram-ring in the Sarkandaugava suburbs.

Pinya, Anninya and I took the number five tram which ran around the Daugava River. Finally, we reached the ring, but I did not recognize the area because, as the driver explained to us, the tram route had been extended. We decided to go back until we recognized a familiar landmark. I noticed an area of adjacent apartment buildings. We stopped there.

It was late in the morning when we arrived. The place looked different now in the daylight. I had not been there during the day before and eighteen years had gone by. Nevertheless, I knew that Ivan's flat was in one of the front buildings. I left Pinya outside, while Anninya and I climbed floor after floor and rang bell after bell. No one knew Ivan. I looked out of a fourth floor window into the court yard and saw Pinya talking to a man. He was, probably, asking him if he knew Ivan. The man was forthcoming and pointed to a window on the third floor of a different building, suggesting that Pinya checks out a few apartments where retired employees from the factory lived. We now understood that none of these employees were ordinary people, they all were secret agents. We were standing in the middle of a cement tundra surrounded by brick buildings filled with former KGB. There were nine buildings in all. I felt uneasy about leaving Pinya in the courtyard by himself, but before we went into the next building, I saw the man again, this time coming over to talk to Pinya with a telephone book in his hand. They were looking for Ivan's telephone number, but to no avail. Later, in the privacy of our bedroom we talked about the man whose name was Vladimir. The man confided to Pinya his situation in Riga.

"He told me that he had a round stamp in his passport."

"What does this mean?" I asked.

"It means that he is an enemy to Latvia. This is a new one on me," Pinya said, and continued, "the man said that they want him out of here because he had not been born in Latvia, he will never become a Latvian citizen. Some people have quadrangle stamps which means that they might get citizenship after six years, never him, even though he's been loyal to Latvia since the end of World War II. The conflict between Latvia and Russia still continues. He has no place to go to in Russia and does not belong here either." Pinya held me feeling my fear and we fell asleep. We needed strength for what was to come.

Anninya and I continued our search for Ivan. I was even more determined to find him after I saw the suffering of the Rigans.

A gray-hair woman stood at the opened door. She knew who Ivan was and directed us to the second front building where we had already been before. In a few minutes the same woman caught up with us apologizing for not inviting us into her home for a cup of coffee. To make up for this slight, she accompanied us to Ivan's building. We accepted her generous offer. Now the three of us climbed to the third floor and rang the bell. It was opened by another gray-haired woman. With a smile of welcome, she motioned for us in. Her husband sat on a sofa in a tiny spotless living room. I recognized both their faces, although I could not recall in which department of the factory they used to work; nor did I remember their names. "The were looking for Ivan," the first woman said. I was relieved to hear that Ivan was alive, he was their friend. They knew that he comes home once a week from his summer place. We had to figure out how to see him.

In the meantime I was afraid to leave Pinya outside for so long and asked Anninya to bring him in. I waited for both of them for a while but they did not come. I became worried when finally I spotted them both from the window in the courtyard. Anninya found Pinya, but could not find her way out of this mammoth place. Before we left, Ivan's neighbors promised to contact him and pass on my message to call us at Tanya's place. However, just to protect our find, we decided to leave a note in his mail box. We left the place feeling victorious. I was relieved to be leaving this frightening place. Now we could return to the city and celebrate our success at the "Vec-Riga" Cafe, a name which indicates its location in the charming Old-Riga in part of the city that was being renovated. A new hotel stood on the sight of the once elegant "Otto Schwartz Cafe" which was bombed out during the war, in the back was the small stylish cafe, Vec-Riga. The same pastry recipes were used that had been used for more than fifty years. Of course, we ordered creamschnidts. Anninya took great pleasure being there with us. Unfortunately, most Latvians could not afford this small luxury. For us, the prices were very low compared to the pastry prices in the USA and in Europe. Before we left, we bought two large boxes filled with the finest pastries in Riga to bring home to Tanya.

We would continue to celebrate our day's success with her, with Mark and with Vladik.

****

We have not been at Ambershore yet and we had only four more days left:

"We must go today, or the latest tomorrow," I said to Pinya.

The phone rang; Vladik said that a man was asking for me. It could not be Ivan so soon, I thought.

"Hello," I said in my English habit.

"Hi, chief," a deep voice answered in Russian. Even though I did not recognize his voice, I knew it was Ivan. I had never been his chief, of course, but this was the Russian way of greeting a person you hold in high regard. Once, my destiny lay in his hands; once I would tremble when I had to speak to Ivan on the phone. How time changed things, I thought.

"I am delighted that I found you, I said with excitement."

"So, you did not forget me?" He asked.

"I will never forget you, my dear friend. I am eager to see you."

"Come next to the factory tomorrow."

"Why should I come there? Please, come to my daughter's friend's house to see us tomorrow," I invited him.

"Give me the address and I will be there at noon," he responded in a firm voice.

I was dizzy with joy. I could never imagine that I would arrange a date with Ivan so easily. Tanya and I began to plan the reception. What kind of food and drinks should we buy? What would I say to him? Another phone call interrupted our party planning. This time it was the lawyer from the Consumer Association to inform Pinya that she would be arriving tomorrow to draw a document for the sale of the store.

Our trip to Ambershore had to be canceled: we did not have enough time, except for a short tour of the city.

The first site I wanted to see was the railroad station, which has been the most important landmark in my life. Twice I was lucky to escape from there, both times for different reasons, but each time for survival. We proceeded to the Latvian University, another important place, an excellent institution in which our daughters, Anechka and Evinka, received their education, though not without pain. This time, the old struggle did not bore me anymore, I was full of pride for their achievements. The small bridge over the narrow canal across the street diverted my attention from the university. Together with Pinya I walked over and stopped in the middle of the bridge to watch the silent swans move lazily through the water. My heart filled with joy, remembering our granddaughter Shulamit, then twenty-months old, pointing her sweet finger to the graceful birds...and then the frightening thoughts entered my mind. What-if we had remained in Riga, what if we had given in to our powerlessness? What if I had not found Ivan? I pushed the questions out of my mind.

It was for Shulamit, for Gabriella, for Ruben, for Naomi to live in the free world. I will never have to ask "What if" again.

****

Pinya and I had to meet the lawyer, therefore Tanya arranged the party for Ivan without my help.

Rasma, a plain looking young woman said with an outstretched hand. "Mr. and Mrs. Gurevich." Her handshake was limp and cool. She seemed friendly at first, but there was an insincerity behind her smile. It was as if she were in duplicity with her boss Inara. She came without the papers we needed to close the transaction, and everything she told contradicted whatever Inara had told us a few days before. I became suspicious whether Pinya will get his property back. We talked for a long time before reaching a decision. Finally, it was agreed upon that a notary should prepare and certify the necessary papers for us. The lawyer insisted that I arrange an appointment with the notary. An appointment was scheduled for us only one day before we were leaving Riga. There was nothing we could do. Now, we had to rush home to welcome Ivan.

As Pinya and I reached Tanya's floor, Ivan was already standing next to her door.

He must have heard my voice from downstairs because when I appeared, he stepped forward and said, "Look, she is even more beautiful than before."

I could hardly see his face in the darkness when I leaned up to kiss him. I think Pinya kissed him too. Needless to say, I had never done that before; our relationship was very official.

"Did you see Lev?" Was his first question.

"No, I was not able to find him." If the reader remembers, Lev Davidovich was the president of the factory whom I went to see at Ivan's suggestion to initiate my release from state security status.

Tanya's door opened before we rang the bell. Introductions were made all around and Tanya invited us to sit down at the festive table. Now in the daylight I could see Ivan more clearly: he had gained weight and looked older. I guessed that he was dressed in his best and only suit. We sat down at the table and I made the first toast to my KGB man.

"To my dear friend Ivan: "Za vstrechu (to our reunion)." We looked at each other deeply, I could hardly hold my tears. Everyone raised their glasses:

"Za vstrechu. Za vstrechu," and we lipped our glasses of the finest French Napoleon brandy.

It took a while for Ivan to loosen up. His silence must have been a habit of his professional training as KGB officer. "Are you happy there?" He asked me with reserve.

"Extremely happy." I answered. I was also reserved about being overly enthusiastic. "I am with my children and grandchildren; I have a good job and a good life. I can be a Jew in the open. I am free."

"How are you feeling now?" He asked, remembering my health problem.

" I am taking medicine which I could not get in the Soviet Union," and stood up to get the packet of Questran to show him.

"How many rooms do you have there?"

"Five rooms besides the kitchen." I answered self-consciously.

"What do you need so many rooms for?" He asked.

"It is common to have a dining room, a living room, a bed room, a den and a guest room." I know this was excessive in comparison with the Soviet style.

Finally, I asked my question which was so many times on my mind.

"Did you know how I found you eighteen years ago?" He answered he didn't know. This time, I doubted his response. As good as I thought he was, I knew him to be, there was always one truth: he was KGB. I told him the story of our adventure, and he accepted it with a nod.

"You have been open with me, so I will tell you something, I helped you because of my wife who said to me after you left our apartment eighteen years ago, Ivan, if a person is ill and is not able to get medicine here, you have to help her get out so that she could find cure. She was a good person,"

"Was?" I asked.

"She died five years ago. I was never going to remarry; no one could take her place, but someone found me: a good woman with good children." Ivan changed the subject. "It was hard, this process of getting you out...all the documents you needed. But I found a way." I waited for him to continue, and he anticipated my question. "Let's leave it at that," he said.

Tears came to my eyes. In my heart I never stopped thanking him.

Ivan called me the next day with Lev's telephone number. He offered to come to the airport to see us off, but I knew he had to travel for hours from his summer place and I didn't want to impose this on him: he had done enough. We said our goodbyes on the phone.

****

Lev Davidovich was known in Riga as one of the most experienced business leaders. Besides being well connected, he was very knowledgeable, well organized and highly respected. With the fall of the Soviet regime in Latvia, Lev, as it was for many other leaders, lost his previous glory. Even though his business skills were suited for any political system, the decline in Latvia's economy forced him out. In my memory he remains a powerful and forceful boss.

Our taxi stopped on Zaubes Street, which was in the most prestigious districts in Riga. Lev waited for us outside. Eighteen years did not diminish his confidence or his robust demeanor. I still noticed that something had changed. Our embraces were heartfelt. Lev took us upstairs to his apartment decorated with art deco furniture, rugs, paintings and exquisite crystal vases. His wife Irina, a physician, received Pinya and me as if we were family. Soon their daughter, her husband, and bursting with vigorous red-headed twins (a boy and a girl) arrived. I could still sense trouble; the family had been denied Latvian citizenship, they missed their chance to emigrate twenty years ago. Would they take the right steps now? We left their home with broken hearts.

There Is No Better Place Than Home

Next day, our last in Riga, we had an appointment to meet Rasma, the lawyer, to sign the papers in the notary's office. Mark was waiting for us on the street with a message that she had called to tell us that she would not be there because her car broke down, and she couldn't get another car, but she would come the following day. I knew it was a ploy.

Although we were loath to call her, we still dialed the number. She knew that we were leaving the next day, she said, and promised, "no matter what," to be there before we had to leave, and bring all the documents which would only have to be certified with Pinya's, hers and notary's signatures.

And so she appeared, two hours before we had to depart for the airport. Together, we rushed to the notary office. It was our good luck that the line was long enough for Pinya to be able to read the document carefully. He left the line, handed the papers back to the lawyer and said, " I will not sign this document. It is a sham."

We made it to the airport just as the plane was about to take off. A few hours later we were safe in Copenhagen. From there the strong Atlantic winds carried us back home.

I took Pinya's hand. "Look down, my dear," I said. "Boston Harbor."

He responded with a kiss. "Mazal Tov, my Rodinkah. I told you that you would have your Chai celebration in the United States. I always keep my promises."

That was on August 17th, 1994.

****

We could see our children waiting for us behind the glass doors.

****

www.ingramcontent.com/pod-product-compliance
Lightning Source LLC
Chambersburg PA
CBHW022152080426
42734CB00006B/407